LOTHIAN

Edited by Allison Dowse

First published in Great Britain in 2003 by
YOUNG WRITERS
Remus House,
Coltsfoot Drive,
Peterborough, PE2 9JX
Telephone (01733) 890066

HB ISBN 0 75434 205 0
SB ISBN 0 75434 206 9

FOREWORD

This year, the Young Writers' The Write Stuff! competition proudly presents a showcase of the best poetic talent from over 40,000 up-and-coming writers nationwide.

Young Writers was established in 1991 and we are still successful, even in today's modern world, in promoting and encouraging the reading and writing of poetry.

The thought, effort, imagination and hard work put into each poem impressed us all, and once again, the task of selecting poems was a difficult one, but nevertheless, an enjoyable experience.

We hope you are as pleased as we are with the final selection and that you and your family continue to be entertained with *The Write Stuff! Lothian* for many years to come.

Contents

The Poems

Life

Then down that river I wandered,
Silent, sleek, soft,
I drifted like an autumn leaf across the sun drenched sky.

I walked across a babbling brook,
That shone in the morning light,
I thought of all the things in life
Which have caused me great pain.

The birds twittered in the trees,
The sound was calm and gentle,
I felt the air lift me to the sky
And drift me further away.

I walked and walked till I was far away,
Deep in thought I caught a glimpse of the morning dew,
Taken aback, a breath very strong,
I knew then life would be fine,
And if I want, all mine!

Vikki Steven (16)
Dunbar Grammar School

Joy

Joy's colour is bright yellow,
It tastes like sweets
and smells like air.
Joy looks like fun,
the sound of laughter.
Joy feels like a calm wind.

Graeme Crawford (12)
Dunbar Grammar School

ANGER

It is like a red face steaming out of smoke.
It tastes like burnt toast.
It smells like a house on fire.
It looks like a red bull chasing you.
It sounds like a steaming train.
It feels like something burning inside you.

Abdul Shahnan (12)
Dunbar Grammar School

HAPPINESS

Happiness is like:
The taste of nice, juicy bananas.
It smells of nice ripe lemons.
It looks like a bright yellow star.
It sounds like singing birds.
It feels like joy in my heart.

Linda Bruce (13)
Dunbar Grammar School

ANGER

Anger is dark red,
It tastes like sour grapes,
It smells like bubbling potions,
It looks like bubbling tar,
It sounds like a bone breaking,
It feels like a punch in the face.

Jack Albano (12)
Dunbar Grammar School

Joy

It is multicoloured.
It tastes like a happy cake.
It smells like an air conditioner.
It looks like a good time.
It sounds like a laugh.
It feels like a soft teddy.

Callum Low (11)
Dunbar Grammar School

Joy

Joy is a nice rosy red,
It tastes like the fresh air,
It smells like the fresh flowers,
It looks like lovely fresh flowers,
It sounds like happiness,
It feels like Christmas.

Chris Campbell (12)
Dunbar Grammar School

Happiness

Happiness is a nice rosy pink,
It tastes like strawberries,
It smells like roses and chocolate,
It looks like happiness,
It sounds like birds whistling,
It feels like the best forever.

Siobhan Craig (12)
Dunbar Grammar School

THE HIGHWAYMAN

The highwayman rides fiercely
Over the grassy moor,
He jumps the gorse bushes carelessly,
Turning rich men to poor.

He rides his faithful white mare,
Her name to be precise is Pointed Mace,
He shouts, 'Come unto me if you dare,
But I will mutilate your face.'

Over the cobbles he clatters and clangs,
'Woahing' his horse to a stop.
He fires his musket with the loudest bang,
Then he runs off *clip clop*.

As he races down an alley,
He is caught around the waist by a rope,
Then dragged off to the nearest chalet,
Hearing voices saying, 'What a dope.'

Battered, beaten, bashed and a-banging,
The highwayman was caught,
Voices saying, 'How about a hanging?'
Others say, 'Slit his throat.'

A conclusion was made that very same day,
That there was to be a town hanging,
He was going to die with no delay,
Unless he started planning.

That morning, when dawn had broke,
The highwayman had gone.
All that was left in the cell was his cloak,
The highwayman lives on.

Caitlin Clutton (13)
Dunbar Grammar School

HALLOWE'EN

'Twas upon one Hallowe'en
My friends and I went out
We heard the most ear-piercing scream
From a well known lout.

We ran to see what was wrong
He pointed to a house
He told us all to watch our backs
For there was a killer mouse.

'Very funny,' we all joked
We were laughing like clowns
This made the lout feel very provoked
Amidst our little town.

He went away and summoned out
The biggest, fiercest beast
And it was its lucky day
For it got a whopping feast.

First went Caitlin in its mouth
Followed by Siobhan
Then it ran off to the south
Distracted by a fawn.

I was left petrified
Where were my friends?
I dropped to the ground and just cried
Then went to search round all the bends.

Still, to this very day
My friends have remained lost
But still they will return I pray
In my memory they are embossed.

Kirsten Thomson (13)
Dunbar Grammar School

THE BANK ROBBERY

The bank doors opened after nine,
A normal day, nothing strange.
Everything seemed to be just fine
But that was all about to change.

The first one burst in through the door!
He held a gun in his hand,
Quickly followed by two more.
What happened next had been well planned.

The leader shouted, 'On the floor!'
His men pulled out two sacks
And knelt down at the safe door,
As he looked down at our backs.

'Hurry guys,' he urged them on,
As they turned the combination.
'No one move, we'll soon be gone.'
I prayed in desperation.

The door opened in a flash.
'Let's move it!' he commanded.
The bags were loaded with the cash.
'Get it all!' his voice demanded.

The robbers sped off down the road
As quickly as could be,
But they would never have known the code
If it hadn't been for me.

Naomi Busteed (13)
Dunbar Grammar School

Love

Love is the colour of romantic red
And tastes like juicy strawberries.
It smells like beautiful roses
And it looks like love.
It sounds like a big sloppy kiss
And it feels like happiness.

Ashley Stewart (12)
Dunbar Grammar School

Anger

Anger is bright red
And tastes like blood.
It smells like dirty water,
It looks like ripped money,
It sounds like a smack,
It feels like your heart has stopped.

Kristofer Bell (11)
Dunbar Grammar School

Reflection

As the water ripples and the golden reflection glows,
The beauty of the palace grows and grows.
As it shines in the dark, brown sky,
The mood is calm, not a sound passes by.
The trees stand tall and quiet at night,
As the palace beside them shines out so bright.
The reflection in the lake doesn't stay for long -
After the sun rises you'll find it's gone.

Emma Watt (13)
George Heriot's School

Happy Times

Stretching and groaning as he strains to get up.
Tiny feet padding gently on the floor.
Grinning joker's face as he bounds along the path,
Gazing straight at me with his adoring eyes,
Tongue lolling out the side of his mouth
As he pants from all the exercise.
Running around in circles trying to catch his non-existent tail,
Chasing little elusive pools of light as they skirt around the room.
Awaking the dormant wildlife as he trudges through the woods,
Stopping abruptly only to sniff the interesting smells
That haunt the forest,
Bouncing over the bracken as he leaps in breathing fields.
The reassuring lick on my hand, reminding me he's there -
Memories of happy times with my old friend Hector.

Ross Collinson (13)
George Heriot's School

Time

Time, it's eternal, it continues forever,
It passes us by, stopping never.
It's continually ticking the years away,
Seconds, minutes, hours, days.

It crumbles mountains, it reshapes the land,
It ruins towns that once were grand.
It drinks up oceans, it devours beasts,
On every living creature, time will feast.

Old Father Time looks down upon us,
Watching us from the stars above.
Only he decides when our lives are done,
And he won't make an exception for anyone.

Kathryn Alexander (12)
George Heriot's School

The Tattoo

The air is filled with colour.
How the Tattoo glows!

People in red ruby, violet-blue coats,
With the gleam of the castle.

The darkness of the sky,
It's quiet, but then it is lit up by . . .
The Tattoo!

Happy, loud music
Puts a joyful smile on all.
Everyone's face is so still
Like they were in a trance.
The Tattoo!

David Kemp (12)
George Heriot's School

The Snail

I watch the day go slowly by,
Sitting in my shell, so very shy,
My shell keeps me safe from all things,
Especially those birds that sing.

Slithering around for a place to hide,
Looking for food with mouth open wide,
Slowly I emerge from my cosy den
And explore the world (and the chicken pen).

Oh help, here I go, my life has come to an end,
The chickens have taken me, no longer to mend,
No longer do I make a sound, let alone a wail,
Who am I? Of course, that little dead snail!

Rebecca Harris-Evans (13)
George Heriot's School

The Lonely Hedgehog

The lonely hedgehog lumbered along,
Listening to a bird's sweet song.
Then the hedgehog cried aloud,
'Why can't I be like a cloud?

I could float around all day,
Watch my troubles drift away.
I could speak to all the birds
And listen to their tuneful words.'

As a hedgehog he despaired,
Everyone of him was scared,
For every time that they came near,
He would prick them like a spear.

'Ouch!' they'd cry and squeal in pain,
'I'll never touch an 'og again!'
And off they'd run, their fingers sore
And he was left alone once more.

Christopher Wickes (13)
George Heriot's School

Mr Fox

I would love to fulfil my dream,
to see a fox with a silver gleam.
I'd love to see your bushy tail,
to make me gasp it would not fail.
I'd love so much to give you a cuddle,
though I am sure you would run in a muddle.
Foxy, foxy, come and see,
how nice it would be if you were with me.

Greg Todd (12)
George Heriot's School

Life

Life starts when a baby is born,
it ends when an old person dies.
Life starts in blissful ignorance,
and ends when we become wise.
Just as we have sorted out,
in our hearts and in our heads,
what life's journey is all about,
we are confined to our beds.
A baby that has just been born,
knows not of the troubles we face,
though ignorance, we regard in scorn
it may be a saving grace.
So what is life, with its fickle ways,
and its many twists and turns?
Is it just a way to pass our days,
or a lesson that we must learn?

Natasha Donald (13)
George Heriot's School

What Is A Rainbow?

As colourful as nature,
As inspiring as the paintbrush itself,
The rainbow is predictable and endless.
A splash of colour in the sky,
A sigh of hope to those who might need it most.
The rainbow is a wonderful and bright event.
The rainbow is joyous, but will fade away.
As you are not able to limit or hold the rainbow in your hands,
It will move on,
Where the sun and rain meet.

Andrew Bell (11)
George Heriot's School

FACE

Lone grey eyes in a face of pain
skin translucent and dark with rain
listen, look, lie low, diffuse
forget about the scarred face blues
and black skin burned along the bone
broken emotions never shown
remember life in a hospital room
a choking stink-of-hate cocoon

the acrid sting of belt on back
spine bruised and tortured, ridged rack
lifelong images of hate and rage
burning to take leave of the depression cage
leave you twisted, broken - in summers, winters -
memorabilia of a face in splinters.

Louise Levicky (13)
George Heriot's School

THE SWEET

It looks like a lemon bonbon,
but believe me it isn't.

As the sweet shows a bit of a glitter,
it sure gives out a taste really bitter.
As the sourness explodes,
it feels like a paradise.

As it sticks to my mouth and fingers,
it feels like honey from a bee.

As the burst of sourness and enjoyment
flows through my mouth,
I can always guess that it is a sherbet lemon!

Stuart Langlands (11)
George Heriot's School

The Lemon Bonbon

The bonbon looks like a full moon in the late night sky,
Where drunks, clubbers and late night people go by.
Then there's the yellow powdered moondust on top
And the uneven surface with craters so deep.
The bonbon is fine and a sensation to eat.
I suck the dust to minimize the size,
Leaving a rough, small sphere cold and unwise.
The dust makes your tongue go wild,
It makes your tastebuds ecstatic and stand on tail's end.
Chewy, sticky and succulent is the tasty treat inside.
It could last a lifetime,
That's if you can't resist sinking your teeth into it.
Then it's gone, down your mouth in a big, deep pit.
All that's left is the brilliant taste in your mouth of the bonbon,
A fantastic, classic, scrumptious sweet.

Jacob Ferguson (12)
George Heriot's School

The Shadows

I look out my window, what can I see?
A grey misty morning as still as can be.
Many people, all rushing around,
Each one with a purpose, not making a sound.
I sit here and wonder, where might they be going?
I could guess for hours, I'll not end up knowing.
I look at the trees, they stand high and tall,
I watch little cottages, that old branches maul.
The red setter and retriever, all bright coloured dogs
Are reduced to grey shadows in the mid morning fog.
I'm feeling so grey. I'm feeling so tired,
I think I'll lay down my pen, and retire.

Rebecca Cherry (13)
George Heriot's School

Winter Season

People come out in the morning air,
They come to see a beautiful sight.
As sights such as this are rarely seen
In the cold, frosty winter season.

From the icy, cold lake to the misty,
tall mountains,
Complete peace and stillness.
The plants, the trees, the rocks,
All frost covered and motionless in the
harsh winter wind.

A cruel mist hanging over the snow-
covered trees and hills.
Everything in complete peace and
stillness,
As sights such as this are rarely seen
In the cold, frosty winter season.

Omair Iqbal (12)
George Heriot's School

The Snow Queen

Layers of ice and melting sleet,
Build up on the lonely cobbled street.
Frozen leaves become crisp and fragile,
Gathering in clumps along the hilltop mile.

Windows to become magically misted,
Soon, the children must wrap up warm - that will be insisted.
The days are colder now and the light is spare,
For this it seems the darkness does not care.

Present evenings become noticeably short,
Families return quickly to their warm, humble forts.
Fires are lit, their bright sparks glowing,
The children no longer shiver as the heat is growing.

Winter has reached the tiny town,
It seems the Snow Queen has come to be crowned.
Soon the sleeping townfolk will wake up to a surprise,
As the falling snow settles and around them lies.

Emma Sinclair (13)
George Heriot's School

WITH THIS HAND . . .

With this hand I scribbled quickly,
My hand racing along the page,
I was writing as fast as I could.
My hand looped in and out,
Carefully shaping the page.
I was thinking about imaginative words,
My brain working as fast as my hand,
My hand ever so slightly jumping
Every few seconds, it was like a kangaroo!
After a few seconds, even hours,
I laid down my pen.
I heard a sigh of relief,
I'd finished my English essay!
My hand was slightly numb with pain
From the hours of work.
I knew it was worth it though,
Because my essay would be dazzling.

Christina Chalmers (11)
George Heriot's School

My Sweet Sensation

Rampageous rhubarb rock, a peaceful delight,
Utterly sour and sweet and still is holey,
The taste to me is red, I wonder why that is,
Even though it's a sweet, you can taste the vegetable
and the artificial taste,
Like a stack of dominoes waiting to be knocked down.

Fantabbydosy fruit creams, jumping on the trampoline,
The cream is smooth, like marble,
No fruit in a fruit cream makes it a bit of a con,
It melts in your mouth and I can sometimes last only five seconds,
Like a fluffy pillow lying on a soft mattress.

Luscious liquorice bonbons, a strong, serious sweet,
Pungent and black, they need a brave mouth,
Not sweet like fruit creams, more tangy like aniseed,
Hard as rock till you crunch through the outer shell,
Then chewy like toffee,
Like a hard stone lying in a field of grass on a fierce, hot summer's day.

Donald Steven (11)
George Heriot's School

My Tenth Birthday

With this hand I sliced the cake,
You could see the excitement in my eyes.
It was my birthday!
Soon I would open my presents.

Everyone's eyes were riveted on me
Like a predator looking at its prey
And then down went the knife
Past the sugary icing, past the jam
Finally reaching its goal

The cake tasted sweet
My hands were getting messier and messier
I took another slice then another
The sweet taste was luring me in

Then suddenly out of everyone's mouth came
'Happy birthday to you, happy birthday to you . . .'
I was so happy until I realised
I was leaving single figures into double!

Alistair Grant (11)
George Heriot's School

ANGER

A terrible feeling of passionate hate,
Overpowering and dreadful, a feeling so great,
Furious, fierce, powerful and intense,
Against our anger, we have no defence
An experience of fury and of burning pain,
Resentful and fiery, so hard to contain.

Tearing and bitter, it pierces one's soul,
Forceful and pulsing, hard to control,
Enough to make one's body tremble,
Cold white embers it does resemble
Raging, seething, wild, white-hot,
Not an emotion easily fought.

Destructive, blinding, dominating,
Deep and enduring, never abating,
From the streams of annoyance come the angry oceans
Of stormy, violent, tumultuous emotions.

Aja Murray (12)
George Heriot's School

WITHOUT

A river without an ending,
A tree without roots.
A lake without water,
A mountain without a peak.

A school without pupils,
A road without cause.
A child without parents,
A choice without pause.

A gift without gratitude,
A talk without truth.
A smile without meaning,
A kiss without love.

And . . .
A poem without an end . . .

Sarah Lyall (12)
George Heriot's School

THE CASTLE IN WINTER

All white, all still, all quiet,
The castle stands dull in the stormy sky.
All is covered in snow
The trees stand tall.

The benches are empty, only snow occupies them.
The snow is like a blanket
Laid over the landscape with no sign of life. Deserted.

I hear nothing.
I see trees all crooked and black.
I smell the frost and, as I touch the snow, it crumbles in my hand.

Alan Scrimgeour (12)
George Heriot's School

DURING THE NIGHT

Gone is the sun,
The night has come.
Darkness is here,
We're filled with fear.

Down in the abandoned wood,
Animals savagely hunt for food.
No longer do the seagulls screech,
Beside the long, deserted beach.

Ghosts sneak around,
Knowing they'll never be found,
Because no one is sure,
Where these dark spirits lure.

Departed has the night,
On the arrival of the light.
Here is the sun,
The morning has come.

Nicola Shand (13)
George Heriot's School

THE WIND

The wind is an invisible man dancing in the trees,
A flock of whirling birds picking up anything it can find,
It is God's breath blowing out candles,
A girl whispering to the sky,
It is a cloud's sneeze,
A steam train of the gods' whistling along,
It is a breath that trees and leaves follow,
An everlasting song.

Emma North (11)
George Heriot's School

'Yesnaby' - An Orkney Poem

Loud, crashing waves,
    The barren, rugged rock.
Still this rock stack stands,
    Separated over time.

The turquoise sea is alive,
    Digging at the cliff.
But this rock stack won't move,
    And still remains standing.

The sky torn open,
    As bright as it can be.
Clouds gather in the distance,
    Maybe, heading towards the sea.

This island will not be forgotten, though,
    For it's still a popular resort.
But will it keep its shape?
    And will it stand much longer?

Aaron Dudgeon (13)
George Heriot's School

What Is Rain?

Rain is a river flowing down from sky
It is the tears of angels, when they start to cry.
A well being emptied in the courtyard of Heaven
It is Scotland's wake-up call at half-past seven.
It is the beverage of the gods, donating some to Earth
It's the baptism of a giant, just after birth.
Rain is magic, transforming to hail
It leads us through our life,
As we follow its trail.

Jamie Irvine (11)
George Heriot's School

The Castle In Winter

The castle stands lonely in the background,
The gardens lying still on their own;
The benches are alive with emptiness but with no heart,
The trees standing barren on the carpet of snow.

In the background the castle stood all alone,
Its roofs partially covered in snow,
The flag flying high in the grey, winter sky
And the trees also covered in snow.

The trees, they stand all in a row,
In the days leading up to Christmas,
Everyone's inside getting prepared,
Leaving the castle and gardens all on their own.

James Peters (12)
George Heriot's School

Origin Of Sin

A sweeping cloak of fear,
Destroying all its shadow covers,
Sewing its dark seeds,
Watering its roots,
Nurturing its evil.

There are others,
But this has the greatest needs.
It comes at you, will consume you.
The choice, a dance with the Devil,
Flirting with sin.

You feel the fear,
Of a child afraid of the darkness.

David Graves (13)
George Heriot's School

War Vs Peace

Peace is like a rose,
Lifeless upon the ground,
War is like a blazing fire,
Flaring all around.

The rose is scrumpled and ugly,
Ignored by passers-by,
The fire is not put out,
However much we try.

Peace is weak and fragile,
No strength to show its face,
War is strong and tough,
Getting faster, picking up its pace.

The rose is caught for but a glimpse,
Before being thrown away,
The fire scares off men, women and kids,
Perched waiting for its prey.

However, deep inside,
We all hope to see peace one day,
As for war,
The destroyer of lives, please don't stay.

Amani Khader (13)
George Heriot's School

Atlantic Puffin

The sadness on the puffin's face will fill your heart with sorrow,
But behind his sadness you see his courage.
As he flies around the sea with elegance and beauty,
The coolness of the winter flows through his wings.

Through the cold winter snow the puffin's beak stays bright,
Like a shining light.
The sleek puffin's beak has multicoloured streaks;
The black and white of its feathers help it through all types of weather
Until the spring returns.

Nick Wilson (13)
George Heriot's School

HANDS

With these very hands I caught the rough ball in the line-out,
Passed it out to the wing with a long sweeping motion.
Everything in slow motion, my heart racing.
Then . . . *impact!*
The breath rushed out of me as the bony shoulder of the academy prop dug into my stomach.
Flat on my back and gasping for breath,
I was as defenceless as a soldier without a rifle.
All I could do was lie and watch as my teammates were tackled
And driven back towards our own try-line.
Suddenly I felt a surge of strength and confidence.
I sprang to my feet and ran over to the maul on the other side of the pitch.
After much struggling and ripping with my hands,
I pulled the mud-smeared ball from the opposition's grasp -
I took my chance.
With around 30 seconds of the match remaining I broke into a sprint.
I also broke the defence.
The amount of adrenaline rushing through me was astonishing.
Try! I slammed the ball onto the wet, muddy grass and heard my teammates cry out in triumph.
We had won!

Tom Raitt (12)
George Heriot's School

The Pineapple Chunk

As hard as a rock yet as sweet as a nut.
As light as a feather but still full of flavour.
Bursting with sugar but still brings you pleasure.
As yellow as the sun but as cold as a freezer.
It sounds, when you're eating, like a giant crunching
Through leaves, branches and strawberry bushes,
A crunch of an ivy leaf, a crash of a branch.
Then it downsizes to those tiny little parts in your mouth.
A burst of flavour reaches your mouth, first slowly but
then it hits your taste buds.
It's a blast of sugar, small, select, tiny cube,
Which comes in packets, a sweet shop or a tub.
Who would have thought that all that flavour
Could be bundled into one tiny, yellow, miniature cube?

Naomi Fleming (12)
George Heriot's School

Linlithgow Palace

The night is still, there is no wind.
The landmark stands high above the tall trees,
All lit up beautifully at night,
With the natural scenery.

The peaceful waves lapping up on the bank,
The two rifles propped up like a crown,
The lake holds the blurred reflection of the palace,
As the hours go on forever.

In 1746 the burning took place after
The '45 rebellion failed.
The decoration has gone, the palace is ancient,
But life goes on in this old palace.

Andrew Robb (12)
George Heriot's School

THE MOUNTAIN HARE

Silver-white powder
Under paw,
Eyes and ears alert to danger,
Movements that are quick and graceful.
A flick of a whisker
She disappears
Down her winter burrow.
White as snow and just as lovely,
What a sight to meet the eye:
Eyes of amber, coat of white,
A beautiful animal
But free and lovely in its home.
In the mist of winter heather
There she is,
The mountain hare.

Iseabail Farquhar (12)
George Heriot's School

WHAT IS A LEAF

A leaf is a magic carpet
Flying high and low

A leaf is the calmest cruiser
Bobbing gently up and down on the waves

A leaf is a flying island
Landing wherever it pleases

It cures the sick
And helps the wounded

A leaf is everything.

Anna Harris-Evans (11)
George Heriot's School

My Wonderful Hands

My hands are really wonderful things.
They're like a dream, all tingling,
But as the dreaded day drew near,
They started wobbling and filled with fear.

When I started I seemed to see
This was fun and filled with glee.
But as I put my pencil down,
I realised it was time to frown.

From these words what can you tell,
Here it comes, the finishing bell.
What was this wonderful time you say,
It was in English, my first ever senior one essay.

Sean Cross (11)
George Heriot's School

My Fingers

My fingers clutch the pen,
But there is little hand control,
I drag the pen towards me,
Then shove it away again,
I hear the pen squeak,
Like a trapped and terrified mouse.
The lines won't go straight,
They wobble
And wiggle out of control
But the lines can be used
Placed in the picture,
The image that will hang,
For an eternity,
Up on the kitchen wall.

Sarah McLean (12)
George Heriot's School

With My Hand . . . Drawing A Picture

With my hand, I took my pencil,
and the sheet of paper too
and started to draw my shoe.
The scratching of the pencil,
the scrubbing of the rubber
I glanced at my shoe, desperately,
as my hand flashed across the paper,
scoring deep, dark marks, that were my picture.
I sighed as I looked at my masterpiece,
and to my surprise, it all turned out well,
the praise from the teacher, I thought was great
and as I left the classroom,
I felt very pleased,
with my drawing of a shoe.

Martin Chambers (12)
George Heriot's School

What Is A Cloud?

The gods' bedtime story, revealed in the sky,
As fluffy as fleecy white lambs, for cherubs flying by,
The cloud is a chameleon, changing colour as the sun
    Goes
        Down . . .

. . . A tiny pinprick in a sea of blue,
As if it is whipped eggs, as white as can be,
. . . Gradually darkening like someone
Pushing it into an unseen prison,
They float around and then, then
They paint a picture, ready and equipped
For the next day . . .

Fiona Johnston (11)
George Heriot's School

Hands And Feet

I found myself at the end of the pier
Tired and worn out.

I dropped down and let my feet rest in the water.
Hanging in the water my feet look strangely distorted.

My feet are buffeted by the seas mighty waves to and fro
The creeping coldness numbing, tingling.
Now I can't feel my feet.

The constant movement of the waves
Give my feet a strange life of their own.

Whilst I'm soaking in the sunlight and heat,
My feet swell, cold, blue, cadaver-like,
It is like I can feel life and death at the same time.
Oh! How strange these feelings are.

Johnny Watt (12)
George Heriot's School

A Day's Catch

As the osprey circles above looking for its prey
The fish swim peacefully unaware.
The osprey sees it now and starts
To dive -
Still swimming, the fish does not know it could die.
Diving at high speed
The osprey has almost reached its goal -
Slash, the bird's claws go in
Its wings beat, keeping it airborne,
The fish in the claws, struggling to get free.
The big osprey flies home with food to feed its young.

Andrew Hume (13)
George Heriot's School

The Big Game

The court lights shone brightly,
Our team name was bellowed out of the speakers
As we ran on to the court,
We had a glimpse at our opponents;
The game was going to be tough,
Before long, we were coming to the last ten minutes,
Someone passed me the ball
Past four of the rivalling team members,
One stood blocking my path.
I felt a sensation of victory,
Passing through the ball and into my hands,
I let the ball fly out of my hands
Like a jet zooming off from its runway,
Swish! The ball crashed through the net,
The final whistle blew, I jumped in the air with joy!

David Clark (11)
George Heriot's School

What Is The Sea?

The sea is a giant bath tub
Swirling bright and clear.
The sea is the million teardrops
Of all the world's worries.
The sea is a cosy blanket
Surrounding all the land.
The sea is a happy gurgling friend
Playing with your feet until the day ends.
The sea is an angry roaring monster
Plunging, leaping, tearing and sweeping.
The sea is a clear pane of glass
Calm and smooth, still as the grass.

Hazel Reid (11)
George Heriot's School

WITH THIS HAND . . .

Slowly, cautiously, I patted the furry bundle with my hand.
Nervously, warily, I picked up the tiny body.
Trustingly, lovingly, it snuggled against me.
Certainly, confidently, I chose him.
This creature was so delicate, so dependent upon me.
Me!
Suddenly, I loved this helpless soul.
Blissfully, ecstatically, I carried him out to the waiting car.
My hands cradled him lovingly, almost as if he was a priceless glass.
To me, actually, he was more than that.
Safely, securely, holding him close to me.
Proudly, protectively, I showed him his new home.
With bright eyes, he stared in fascination about the living room.
Tail in the air, he snuffled and sniffed silently around his new residence.
Joyfully, delightedly, that is how I chose my dog with this hand.

Catriona Bertolini (12)
George Heriot's School

WHAT IS WIND?

Wind is a breath from Heaven,
A sigh rippling the sea,
A calm breeze is like a dolphin,
Breaking the surface of the water
Then diving down,
A tornado is the siren of an ambulance
Getting louder and louder
Then fading away,
Clouds in a gale are like paper in
The fire melting away.

Tom Laverick (11)
George Heriot's School

Snowdream

I drew back the curtains - what a surprise!
A large white blanket in front of my eyes.
No warning, unheralded, 'knee deep' they said,
I rushed back and quickly made up my cosy bed.

'You must put your hat on, you'll get frostbite,'
The front door opens - what a magical sight.
Oh hurry, hurry - it might suddenly melt,
The harsh, biting wind is all that I felt.

Glistening, sparkling, ice-cold snow,
Layer by layer, row by row.
Where did it come from, just overnight?
It feels so soft, fluffy and light.

I build a snowman, bit by bit,
Then by a snowball, I am hit.
What a wonderful day this is going to be,
All this snow is just for me!

I bring out my sledge and go for a ride,
After a while, I go back inside.
How warm and cosy it is in here,
But sadly, my bedtime is drawing near.

I go back outside for just a minute
In my hat, scarf and woolly mitts.
Oh no! But how? My snowman has gone
And the snow is no longer carpeting our lawn.

I switch on the radio, while cosy in bed,
Against my white pillow, I rest my head.
Suddenly, I jump and feel no more sorrow,
'There will be snow here again tomorrow!'

Emily Frier (12)
George Heriot's School

THE MOUNTAIN HARE

Snow like glitter,
Thick on the ground,
Trees so dense,
All around
And a cold, so harsh,
But not a sound.
The pines ever tall,
Their heavy perfume,
Hanging in the air.
Their green making shadows,
Deep and dark.

The mountain hare,
Its eyes cautious,
As quick as silver,
In every move, there is care.
Its ears sharp,
Alert for the slightest sound.
Its nose twitching,
For the scent of danger.
Its fur ivory-white,
Hard to see
Against the glaring snow.
Its paws finding grip,
On a gripless surface.
Its legs steady,
Ready for flight.

Helen Lockwood (13)
George Heriot's School

With This Foot I . . .

With this foot I scored a goal,
A goal for me and for the team.
It was breezy and brilliant
And the sun was out for us.
As we proudly walked on the pitch,
The sun flashed upon the ball.
The first few minutes flew by
And we could see it would be a struggle.
Then, just by chance,
The ball touched my foot.
I ran towards the goal,
The giant behind the posts glared at me.
I kept running,
I stopped,
Looked around
And like a film in slow motion,
I took a large kick at the ball.
It flew through the air
Like the most beautiful bird.
The net went back as the ball went in
And the whistle blew.
The game was over.
We had won!
We marched off the pitch like heroes!
My feet were tired and sore
But they held on and supported me
'Cause they knew we had won!

Kirstyn Gleeson (12)
George Heriot's School

Billy Goat's Rough

The wild goats play in the freshly laid snow,
Rolling, running free and fighting,
No cares in the world, snow-splattered faces.

One day Billy Goat wandered free,
Away from the commotion of the herd, he went,
Down to the litter-strewn road.

Cars flying past him, swishing tyres,
Out flew a large bottle of Pepsi,
Smacking him right between the eyes.

Billy staggering back to the herd,
Stumbling through the snow-covered grass,
Falling down in front of his friends, feeling a bit of an ass.

'Oooh, Billy Goat's rough!'

Pete Walls (13)
George Heriot's School

What Is A Rainbow?

What is a rainbow?
A rainbow is the sky's heart, beautiful to mankind
A rainbow is a coloured ribbon you can't hold
A rainbow is the gateway to Heaven
A rainbow is coloured pencils dropped in a cool stream
A rainbow is God's love brilliantly shining in all the
dark corners of the world
A rainbow is ink spilt on a pale blue page.
What is a rainbow?

Matthew Lyall (11)
George Heriot's School

My Hands

With my hands I picked up the club
Which glimmered in the sun,
As I placed the ball down,
It seemed to be like a star in a green universe.

When I stood up I took my aim,
(A small tree in the vast fairway).
I stared, how am I meant to win,
I must have looked like a rabbit in a car's headlights.

As I swung back,
My feeble hands slipped.

The second I hit the ball
I knew I had fluffed the shot.
I let my hand shield my eyes from the blazing sun,
In hope of finding my lost ball.

Graham Dickson (12)
George Heriot's School

Sweets, Wonderful Sweets

Some sweets are chewy, some sweets are soft,
Some sweets are made to help if you cough.
I prefer red sweets, I don't much like green,
The dentist says I can't have any, isn't that mean!
Chewy, stripy humbugs, sparkling fruit gums,
Big bags of assorted toffees to share with my chums.
Mars bars, Sherbet Dabs, Mojos, Flakes,
All different flavours, all different makes.
Some people like liquorice allsorts, some people like mints,
When it's my mum's birthday, she likes chocolates, she hints.

Colin Glancy (12)
George Heriot's School

Standing Stones

How did they get there?
Nobody knows.
How did they get there, 53 pale grey stones?
Were they put there on purpose or did they just fall?
So quiet and peaceful I can't even tell.
The sky a deep blue, the grass a light green,
With small yellow buttercups - that's all I can see.
I take a look around, then standing in front of me
are 53 pale grey stones
staring back at me,
so jagged and tough; they look so hard to touch.
Then I look to the sky so fluffy and peaceful.
Miles from anywhere,
you've got nothing to do but look at the 53 pale grey stones
in a circle in front of you.
They'll be there forever for people to see
53 pale grey stones -
that's what they mean to me!

Abbie Shand (12)
George Heriot's School

Capercaillie

Standing in the grass, wet with dew,
Head held proudly high,
Prancing through the grass:
Green feathered chest,
Red ringed eyes,
Tail feathers sprouting high,
Pointed, spiky rough chin.
With a ring of sparkling feathers
Round its neck glinting in the sunlight.

Rory Downie (13)
George Heriot's School

Sweets, Sweets, Sweets

Sweets, sweets, tangy sweets
All you can eat!
Sweets, sweets, tangy sweets
All you want for a daunt
Sweets, sweets, sweets!

A bonbon is a jubilation
Covered in a sweet sensation
A fruit pastille is like a rascal
Covered in scorching summer sand
Sweets, sweets, sweets!

Sweets - tweets, sweets - tweets
All you want for a real swant
Sweets - tweets, sweets - tweets
Real bomb for a real bomb!
Sweets, sweets, sweets!

Stuart McInnes (12)
George Heriot's School

What Is A Rainbow?

A rainbow is a valley, high in the sky
A waterfall of colour
Cascading through blue rivers
A rainbow is the archway
Leading into Heaven
A sign for peace
That everyone sees
But do they hear?

Natalie Garden (11)
George Heriot's School

FEET - RACE AGAINST TIME

As the sun glinted off car windows,
I looked at my watch.
It was up to me to race against time,
With all the power of my feet
I ran with all my might.
As my mind filled with doubt,
I could feel my feet shaking,
I leapt,
I jumped,
But it was up to my feet to catch that train.
I felt alone and scared as I suddenly stumbled.
As I threw my feet forward,
Other weary feet jumped from my path.
We beat time as my stubborn feet
Beat against the hard concrete.
My heels were raw and my sluggish toes stung,
But finally I sat down
And breathed a huge sigh of relief.
'Until next time,' a voice gasped.

Hannah-Leigh Gray (11)
George Heriot's School

SWEETS

Sweets! Sweets! That's what we eat,
Sugary, tasty, soury sweets.
Fruit pastilles, Skittles, rhubarb and acid and drops
Bonbons, sherbet suckers and pear drops.

We will start off with the sweetless Skittles,
Which makes me think of the smell of pickles,
Pickles! Pickles! Pickles! Pickles!
Yes, those old smelly pickles.

Secondly we've got the really tasty rhubarb rock,
Quick I think of the tick-tock of a clock,
Tick! Tock! Tick! Tock!
Off goes the tick-tock of that clock.

Third and last we've got strawberry bonbons,
Which I'm wanting for tomorrow.
Tomorrow! Tomorrow! Tomorrow! Tomorrow!
Tomorrow they will be gone.

Calum Lobban (12)
George Heriot's School

My Snowy Place

Walking through the forest
Through the crisp, white snow,
The light shines across
The open land.
You see the trees and snow
The trenches of trees and bark.

Snow glistening,
Glistening onto the pebbles.
Footprints crushing the hard ice,
You see the grass rise,
Through the frozen water.

Snow,
Drip,
Drip,
Dripping
On the mountain face -
Oh, how I love this snowy place.

Emma Smith (13)
George Heriot's School

Painting A Picture

My hand lay motionless,
resting on the smooth, reassuring piece of paper.
my fingers tightly wrapped
around the thin paintbrush.
The paint lay still and glistening
in its rusty old palette,
encouraging me to dip the thin bristles
of the brush into the yellow mixture.
Slowly I did just that
cautiously but determined I began to paint.

With swift, graceful movements my hand
turned the dull paper into a masterpiece.
The colours seemed to flow into one another.
The variety of colours was immense
from black to orange, brown to yellow.
I was dazzled by the brightness of it
how proud I was I could not tell
but I owe it to my hands,
without them I do not know where I would be.

Greig Easton (12)
George Heriot's School

My Hand

My hand slides down the rail
As I get into the pool.
As water rushes over me
My body starts to cool.

With this hand I pull myself through the water
Like a turtle swimming around.
With this hand I pull myself through the water
Like a spade digging the ground.

My hand starts to wrinkle
Like a grape when it's old.
My skin gets softer
Like snow when it's cold.

My hand is in and out of the water
Like a dolphin beside a boat.
Sometimes I even feel like a fish
Swimming along, afloat.

Ailsa McKain (12)
George Heriot's School

THE LONG JUMP

These feet have been through a lot,
They have been over tough terrain,
Be it smooth, rough, bumpy or muddy.
Now had come the big day,
When their training comes into use.
In the distance I see the sand,
Into which these feet will plunge.
I stand at the end of the runway.
I breathe deeply, my mind focused
And I'm off, each step seems like a mile,
My legs pump like a steam train's wheels spinning,
My feet hit the ground, *bang, bang, bang!*
And then *thud!* A perfect landing!
Shaken and wobbly my feet stand me up.
They keep me balanced and I wait in suspense.
Has their work paid off?
The tape measure's out . . . the gold is mine!
I now realise my feet are my heroes!

Iain Taylor (12)
George Heriot's School

FEET

Bang!
The deafening starting gun whizzed round my head
like a barbaric buzzing bee.
My heart racing, I set off running up the hill.
The scorching sun followed me in and out of the trees,
Burning my back as I ran.

The finish line was still miles away,
Already my feet were beginning to give up on me.
My feet, being determined as they were carried on steadily.
Turning the corner I saw my friends and family cheering me on.
Convinced I could take over the girl in front of me,
I put on a sprint and succeeded.

The dazzling finish line was in view.
Reaching the top of the hill I let my legs loose,
Running frantically down the hill as fast as my feet could take me,
My legs whirring round and round.
I ground to a halt and collected my card.
22nd.
I hadn't won but to myself I was a winner.
My feet had earned their place.

Laura Henderson (12)
George Heriot's School

WHAT IS A RAIN CLOUD?

A rain cloud is a woolly jumper, torn by the wind,
A wet painting dripping in a cellar,
A pond camouflaged by the night sky,
A broken TV shattering to the ground,
A rain cloud is a gas mask blowing out fumes.

Caroline Collinson (11)
George Heriot's School

Cricketing Hands

I use my hands for playing cricket,
For instance bowling at the wicket.
Getting somebody out by catching,
Running out by throwing.

My hands are fast,
My hands are powerful
Like a great king in his land,
In the cricket field their wrath is vast.

When batting, gloves are used,
To give my hands some help.
Otherwise if they got hit
I would give a great yelp.

Swinging the bat
At the ball
Is like hitting a rat,
As hard as you will.

My hands are commanding
Of the bat
They command like colonels
And defend like rats.

Ehmer Aziz (12)
George Heriot's School

What Is A Meadow?

Looking at a meadow from up high
And seeing a quilt of dazzling colour
A meadow is a cake covered in sprinkles of colour
A meadow is a blanket covering in the Earth
A meadow is a paradise for all around.

Edward Slater (10)
George Heriot's School

PHOTOS

Going on the ferry to France,
Crossing over La Manche
Taking photos with these hands.

Snap, snap,
Snap, snap.

On tour with the tour guide,
Having fun day and night,
The light of the camera,
Making me blind.

Flash, flash,
Flash, flash.

At Arramanches the beach so bare,
The wind blowing in our hair,
Taking photos of my friend Claire.

Click, click,
Click, click.

Having a chat with my friend,
Our holiday had come to an end,
My tired hands,
Driving me round the bend.

Whirr, whirr,
Whirr, whirr.

Beth Thoms (11)
George Heriot's School

My Feet

The starter blew the whistle,
I was off.
The muscles in my feet started working,
Pushing, pulling, pushing, pulling.
My feet continually hit the ground,
Like the feet of a buffalo in a buffalo stampede.
I couldn't do anything about them, they just wouldn't stop.

The conditions were perfect for running,
The sun shone down on the track,
My feet didn't give way once.

My faithful feet were carrying me to the finish line.
The finish line appeared, down the track.
I had to win.
I was in the lead.
My feet did all they could to take me those last few paces,
The hardest few paces in the race.

I looked across,
Yes, I had done it,
I had won!

The race was over,
My feet slowed down, coming to a stop.
I looked down at my feet,
'Thanks,' I gasped.

Philip Pagan (12)
George Heriot's School

What Is A Rainbow?

A rainbow is God's heavenly art set
It's a sight like never before
An arc of friendly colours leading to Heaven
A rainbow represents life
It's like a child painting a picture of Camelot
A utopia
A paradise
A rainbow is like a cat playing with many balls of coloured string
Rainbows are signs in the sky which guide us through life.

James Macfarlane (11)
George Heriot's School

A Cloud

A cloud is a golf ball floating across the sky,
A cloud is an unwanted sheep banished from Earth,
A cloud colours the lonely sky,
A cloud supplies our water,
It covers the moon on dull nights,
It brings our Scottish fog.

Alex Ferguson (11)
George Heriot's School

What Is The Moon?

The moon is a big cookie floating through space,
It is a ten pence lost by another galaxy,
It is a top of a yellow pen that has been thrown up by a naughty child,
It is a blur of colours accompanied by a starry sky,
It is a night light for us down on Earth as we sleep.
The moon is a yellow ball claimed by America.

Jack Kildare (11)
George Heriot's School

Fruit Gums

The green reminds me of the countryside,
The black of the black coal beside the rail.
The red of the dark red seats
And the yellow of the light yellow roof.

They taste soft and fruity,
Full of yummy delight.
The taste can last forever it seems,
When it only really lasts about 3 minutes.

Scott Kennedy (12)
George Heriot's School

What Is A Cloud?

A cloud is a cat's ball of string rolling across a blue carpet.
A cloud is a white paint splodge spread across a blue paint palette.
Clouds are balls of cotton wool wiping off blue face paint.
Clouds are snowballs flying through the air on a winter day.
A cloud is like a swan gliding across a blue pond.
A cloud is a white flower petal away in a summer wind.

Erin Illand (11)
George Heriot's School

What Is A Star?

A star is a floating heaven,
Drifting upon the sky,
Like a raining mountain from up high,
It has a different setting,
No hustle and bustle, no cars rushing.

Cameron Corsie (10)
George Heriot's School

What Is A Sunset?

The sunset is a burst of colour.
As the sun goes down,
The sunset is a painting of the sky,
The sunset is the last resistance,
As the sun disappears,
The sunset is a page of music but,
For the eyes, not the ears,
The sunset is the most beautiful thing,
To cross the evening sky.

Katie Stewart (11)
George Heriot's School

What Is The Earth?

The Earth is a marble stuck in space
The Earth is a spinning ball
The Earth is a boat floating through the darkness
The Earth is both dark and light
The Earth is friendly with the sun
The Earth is never asleep.

Sam Forbes (10)
George Heriot's School

What Is Time?

Time is our wake up call from the rooster,
It is the ringing of the bell at the end of the day,
It is what we need to keep us going.
Without time you would not be reading right now,
For it is our life.

Chiara Donald (10)
George Heriot's School

What Is The Sea?

The sea is a flooded bath covered with salt.
The sea is God's unfinished glass of water.
The sea is a swimming pool as far as the eye can see.
The sea is a basin covering most land.
The sea is a fish tank supporting all fish.

Christopher Droog (11)
George Heriot's School

Ground Swell

(After Edward Hopper, 1939)

As I gaze around, the massive sail
Is first to catch my eye.
It is early afternoon and the sky is bright
As the sun shines on the light blue ocean.
The blue is used throughout.

Changing from light to dark, moving
From air to water, I feel calm.
The gentle sound of the waves is distinctive;
Like peaceful snoring in the ocean's deep sleep.

A group of people sails along the sea
For no obvious reason, besides relaxation,
The abstract shape of the boat,
Like none I've seen before.

Further to the left, I notice
Dolphins playing in the distance.
As I look back towards the boat,
I recognise one of the men
As me, years ago with my friends.

David Ferguson (14)
James Gillespie's High School

Dolphin

(After Jo Shapcott)

You think I'm elegant and intelligent,
Man's special friend.
But I
Pick my nose,
Enjoy a cigarette on the quiet
And play my Game Boy - endlessly.

You think I'm lithe and cheerful,
Paragon of virtue.
But I
Slob out and eat doughnuts,
I lose my temper, shout at friends
And sulk in the depths of the ocean.

Astrid Brown (14)
James Gillespie's High School

Window

On one side of me there is a bedroom,
On the other a garden.
I sit frustrated as I watch
People play, people laugh.
I can't even move
Unless I'm opened to let the outside in.
At night curtains cover me up
As if they are ashamed of me.
At day when no one's around
I stare outside longing to be free.
No one even looks at me.
They just look through me.

Jude Purcell (14)
James Gillespie's High School

The Lion

The lion deep inside me
Roars from within my heart,
As though yearning for freedom.

Pulling at the chains
Always dragging him down,
Longing to run and be free.

Like the fire deep inside me,
Burning yellow and orange,
Raging out of control.

His untamed mane
Is shaggy and tangled,
Yet each hair unique.

The lion is always pulling.
To give up the fight would surely be
To douse the flames inside.

Mhairi McLellan (14)
James Gillespie's High School

She

It's late evening and she's sitting alone, waiting,
People watch, as she fiddles with her hair,
With an empty glass, a box of matches,
Sadness in her eyes,
As she checks her cranberry-stained lips.
She seems so far away.
As the police cars pull up outside,
Sirens sounding, over and over.

Vanessa Boyd (14)
James Gillespie's High School

LION

I am the lion
who lies in the roasting sun
on the baking ground.

The sky is clear
as is the rock-hard ground.
Nothingness stretches for miles.
This is my kingdom.

The odd tuft of greenery
or tree skeleton
provides the only shade
in this dusty landscape.

I lie exhausted and panting
in the heat.
This is my kingdom.

Isaac Turner (14)
James Gillespie's High School

VODKA

I am god of slur,
the daze master.
I have been brewed
to great effect.
My strong sickening taste
destroys all meaning,
reasoning,
feeling.
My after effects are punishing.
The relentless sickening
inspires my educating detention.

Liam Power (13)
James Gillespie's High School

Double Meanings

Words in poems
Double meanings.
A tree's not a tree,
But a symbol of life
Or a dark oppressor,
A pointing finger
Defying the sky.
Personified
It could be a boy
Alone in the world.
Yet what it was
Through the poet's eyes
Doesn't matter.
So now analyse
And forget to enjoy.

Liam Young (14)
James Gillespie's High School

The Feel Of Silk

Is the taste
of a Galaxy bar
melting in your mouth.

A floating feather
drifting to the ground.

The scent of freshly
picked roses
sitting in a vase.

The sound of water
trickling down a stream.

Linda Lashley (14)
James Gillespie's High School

LIFE

(After Jo Shapcott)

My life as an owl
is for seeing
my prey.

If I look long enough
I can see
mice scuttling around
the leafy floor.

If I open my eyes wide enough
I can see
the vicious wilderness.

If I squint strongly enough
I can see
between the barn doors.

I can see
whatever I choose
to see.

Owl death is closed eyes.

Natalie Mackay (14)
James Gillespie's High School

MY CONSCIENCE

My conscience follows me around,
tagging along, annoying me,
constant reminder of my lies,
my faults, my crimes against the world.

As I walk to lunch he follows,
'Tell, tell! Be truthful! Be nice!'
he hisses in my ear.
I can bear that, I just ignore him.

It's at night my conscience is victorious,
he whispers in my ear as I sleep,
a reminder in my dream,
as my lies, my faults, my crimes against the world haunt me.

My conscience always wins,
is always victorious,
and always comes back.

Hannah Wright (14)
James Gillespie's High School

Rose

Over time,
We grow gradually,
Slowly, perfectly.

Making each finger
And toe, separately,
Proudly.

We are loved,
Cared for,
Fed and watered.

Growing a bud
And another.
Opening beautifully.

Then each child
Is taken,
Cut from us.

Each limb,
Broken and torn,
Down to our core.

Hannah Bornet (14)
James Gillespie's High School

Snake

A creature screams out inside me,
Identity unknown, even to itself.
My heart beats, throbbing against my chest,
Like a hammer on a stubborn nail.

I feel it worm its way through my body
Leaving an invisible trail of deceit and lies.
Its forked tongue licks my conscience,
Tantalising. Will it leave or strike me guilty?

He is the snake in me, all that is wrong,
Creeping and flowing through my veins.
I will not let him win.

Kirrily Burns (14)
James Gillespie's High School

Tiger

I am the fire of the jungle,
spreading quietly through the trees.
My teeth are the ragged mountains
whiter than snowy peaks,
grinning as they tear through meat.

My eyes are the night sky,
dark, silver,
mysterious.

The wind is my voice,
tearing through the trees.
With every roar I am shouting,
'Ruler of the Earth!'

Susan Phillips (14)
James Gillespie's High School

SERPENT WITHIN

I can feel it,
The snake inside me
And must do whatever he says.

Quick to anger,
Quick to pounce,
Then he must shed his skin
And start over.

His tongue runs like oil
Off my own
And all I can do is let
Him hiss and spread through me.

Once I have calmed
He returns to the hole
In my heart, waiting . . .

Philip Farish (14)
James Gillespie's High School

WAR MOVIES

The snarling, screaming jaws of bullets,
Embedded in some nameless extra,
Generate a fountain of gasps.
Young, scared men founder
Before the sea of faces.
The audience squirms,
A young man asks why?
Blood on his face
Dirt on his clothes.
Images that scream
Screamed by someone who isn't there.

Jacob Burns (14)
James Gillespie's High School

SPIDERS

(After Jo Shapcott)

There's something I can't feel or hear.
I don't see them yet I know they're there.
It's my emotions calling out.

Now, emotions are a complicated thing
So let's just call them spiders.
You may not understand so let me explain.

At first sight some people are scared or nervous
But you really needn't worry.
If you want the truth, they're more afraid of you.

All day their webs are growing like the thoughts
In my head right now.
They catch ideas like flies.

Where the next one comes from I can't be sure
But no matter what, they fly in unaware.
I devour them whole.

Matthew Deary (14)
James Gillespie's High School

I AM

I am winter with my snow-white coat,
I am Antarctica with its cold dark caves,
I am snow with my polar bear paws,
I am the kitchen, warm and delicious.

I am the boss of ice caps,
I work for myself,
I play the instrument of meat,
My one and only prey.

I am the crunching jaws,
I am the great destroyer,
I am the huge silver truck,
I am the holiday down south.

I am the harsh cold wind,
I am the gleaming white teeth,
I am the fluffy little fur ball,
Who'll bite off your feet.

Sean Murray (14)
James Gillespie's High School

My Magic Box

I will put in my box
never-ending days,
people who fly,
cars as aeroplanes.

I will put in my box
Hibs playing in the Champions League,
my gran Barkat,
money falling from the sky.

My box is fashioned
from sunlight, gold and silver,
with stars on the lid,
and gems on the corners.
Its hinges are the toe of a monster.

I shall run in my box
across the dead sea.
I will float to the other side.

Qasim Ali (13)
James Gillespie's High School

My Magic Box

I will put in my box:

An earthquake that makes buildings,
a fire-breathing snowman,
a constellation of moons.

I will put in my box:

Lips that speak no evil,
trees that grow eggs,
a green sky.

I will put in my box:

A strand of blue grass,
a marshmallow filled pillow,
an inverted tower.

My box is fashioned from starlight and moonlight and silver,
with a horse on the front and flowers in the corners.
Its hinges are the leg joints of the gods.

I shall sail in my box like a cruise ship,
on the calm, Caribbean sea,
then come to a desert island covered in leafy, green trees.

Victor McNeil (12)
James Gillespie's High School

Crocodile

The crocodile inside me is usually quite calm
It glides and lies about and watches life float by,
But when a feeling comes over it,
Like a mosquito biting at its skin
It slaps and snaps and splashes and crashes.

The monkeys screech,
The birds fly,
Animals scatter
Then it stops
And glides away.

Judith McGowan (14)
James Gillespie's High School

My Box

I will put in my box:

Currie flavoured ice cream,
people growing on plants,
stars on the floor.

I will put in my box:

The moon made of cheese,
sun, an ice lolly,
flying cars.

I will put in my box:

Green sky,
black and white rainbows,
rainfall of money.

My box is made of the faces of my good friends,
with each one smiling back at me.

I will fly in my box,
in the green sky,
and end in my house made of soft, fluffy candyfloss.

Najia Chohan (13)
James Gillespie's High School

I Will Put In My Box

I will put in my box:

A tree that grows money,
A rainfall of sweets,
And magical powers for everyone.

I will put in my box:

A huge shopping mall for friends and family.
Everlasting sweets for all the children.
A Disney World too.

I will put in my box:

A multicoloured sky made from sugar,
And a bubblegum flavoured sea,
Maybe Hearts winning the Scottish Cup.

My box is lined in:

Designer clothes and all the trendy and fashionable gear.

The corners of my wonderful box will be made of
gold and all rich things.

I shall fly through the sky and eat my way around.

Then I will settle on my silvery, sugar beach
With all my friends and family.

Dee Heseltine (13)
James Gillespie's High School

My Great Box

I will put in my box:
  the city of Amsterdam,
  the country of Jamaica,
  no laws for people to break.

I will put in my box:
  an everlasting bag of chips,
  a pet snow tiger,
  a ghostly castle all in black.

I will put in my box:
  a flying Lotus Elise,
  invisible grass,
  no cricket or croquet.

My box is lined with gold,
  and there are sheets of ice
  on the lid. Liquid gold runs
  through the corners and the hinges
  are tiger's claws.

I shall eat space-cakes in my box,
  sitting on Amsterdam,
  then drive my Lotus Elise
  to the gates of the ghostly castle.

Sean Lasseur (13)
James Gillespie's High School

WOMAN WITH A PEARL NECKLACE

(After Johannes Vermeer)

The woman with the gold dress
Is the brightest thing in the room.
It is morning,
Fresh light streaming through the window.
Yellow and white
Immediately jump off the picture,
They are cold and gloomy.
The morning light sounds like birds singing.
She looks out of the window with hope in her eyes.
Yet, she still looks sad and lost,
Tying on her pearls, as if waiting to show them to someone.
On the table lies a small scrap of paper,
Maybe containing the words of the person
She waits for.
She keeps her small memories near.

Outside, a carriage pulled by a large grey horse,
Trots up the path.
A maid knocks loudly on her door
And tells her who has arrived.
With a smile on her face, she leaves her room.

The woman with the gold dress
Lights up with happiness
And her lips curl into a smile,
As she runs out to greet him.

Elisabeth Anderson (13)
James Gillespie's High School

Partial Hallucination - Six Apparitions Of Lenin On A Piano

(After Salvador Dali)

Six decapitated heads
of a once-powerful man
lie silently.

It is morning,
but everything is in darkness.

Blackness is all around,
failure is in the air.

I hear the silence
of an unplayed piano.

A frail old man sits away from his friend,
an idealist.

The music book is blank,
desperately in need of rewriting.

To the right
the black expanse develops.

One shall come,
to rethink all that is wrong,

but for now,
it is morning and all is black.

Simon Richardson (14)
James Gillespie's High School

In The Dark

I cannot see, for I am in the dark.
There is a distant bell tolling
and a silent drum rolling.
Twenty-five past four
as light seeps under my door.
I turn the handle
and nothing hits me hard in the face.

The bell tolls thirteen
and I round the corner
moving calmly down the cold, stone steps
my feet absent-mindedly collecting dust on the way.
I pass through a gothic archway
into a dank, dark cavern.

I am immediately immersed
in a black wind of shrieking bats.
I cross the cavern and go through a door on the other side
and I come into a room filled with evil paintings,
containing nothing but hundreds of thousands of
glaring human eyeballs.

All at once I see another image,
that of an eye with wings and a tail.
'Malak' it says in broad gold letters
above this evil thing.
This eye catches mine
and I cannot look away.

Jon Brown (14)
James Gillespie's High School

My Magic Box

I will put in my box

Money that will grow on trees
Breathable water
The heat from the sun.

I will put in my box

Theme parks just around the corner
Floating cars for everyone
The ability to walk on water.

I will put in my box

Flying fish who do your homework
Free drinks for everyone
Discos everyday.

I will put in my box

Sweets for free
A room that tidies itself
Holidays every week.

My box is made out of gold, water and ice
With music on the lid.
Mysterious things on the sides
Its hinges are the petals of red roses.

I shall fly in my box
Over the world and its seas
Then land on an island with the finest pears.

Jade Shand (13)
James Gillespie's High School

My Magic Box

I will put in my box:

A horse riding a jockey,
summers being sunny,
getting paid to go to school.

I will put in my box:

Cats chasing dogs,
cars flying,
planes driving.

I will put in my box:

People only speaking one language,
the sun coming out at night,
the moon coming out at day.

I will put in my box:

Craigmillar Park winning golf trophies,
Rangers and Celtic coming last,
me being the number one golfer in the world.

My box is fashioned from £1 notes, wood and CDs,
with shark's teeth on the lid and surf shops in the corners.
Its hinges are golf clubs, bent.

I shall drive a golf buggy in my box
flip over ramps in the biggest skateparks,
then wake up concussed in a hospital bed with morphine rushing
through my veins.

Gregor Thomas (13)
James Gillespie's High School

Another Box

I will put in my box
The air in my box
The Eiffel Tower
The sun

I will put in my box
Diving whales
My mum
Florida

I will put in my box
Hearts winning the Scottish Cup
Scotland winning the World Cup
Scotland winning the Six Nations

I will put in my box
More-you-eat-thinner-you-get sweets
Flying cars
Blue people

My box is made of
Steel from Sheffield
Fingers for keys
And made of gold

My box is flying overseas
Looking below seeing blue whales
And trawling the moon.

Jamie Murray (13)
James Gillespie's High School

My Box

I will put in my box:

Money growing plants
and large purple mountains
and black and white fire

I will put in my box:

Monkeys for pets
and floating cars
pens that do the work for you.

I will put in my box:

The clouds on the ground
a time machine
people that can breathe underwater

My box will be made of:

Solid gold and silver
with large plated corners
and solid iron hinges

I will put in my box:

Big green tigers and lions
houses made of chocolate and sweets
and pools filled with Coke and Pepsi.

Gavin Smith (12)
James Gillespie's High School

My Magic Box

I will put in my box:

Earthquakes that create buildings
Food would grow randomly
I will put a bigger box in my box

I will put in my box:

Green fire which will burn my money trees
Veggies that taste beautiful
Scotland win the World Cup

I will put in my box:

A waterfall of dogs and
rain will fall from the ground
the moon which will give us sunlight

I will put in my box:

Houses that are as long as air
A room that tidies itself
Food that makes you thinner

My magic box is made from
colourless colours and metal that bends
the sides are made from air but you can't get in
and stars that shine in a whisper

I will travel to Florida
it doesn't rain water, it rains fruit
and where the world is perfect.

Andrew James McCall (13)
James Gillespie's High School

In My Box

I will put in my box:
The feeling at Christmas.
The sparkle of stars.
The brightness of sunlight.

I will put in my box:
No school at all.
Fun that never ends.
Roller coaster rides.

I will put in my box:
Holidays all year.
The laughter of my friends.
The smile of the world.

I will put in my box:
Giant giraffes.
The rustling of leaves.
The colours of the rainbow.

My box is made of silk and silver,
Colours of joy,
Stars and sunlight,
Flowers and fun.

I will swim in my box,
With dolphins and the whales,
And will end up in
The best place on Earth.

Rosie Williamson (13)
James Gillespie's High School

My Magic Box

I shall put in my box:
Scotland getting past the first round
Faroe Islands winning the World Cup,
a blue football pitch.

I shall put in my box:
the endless chants of football fans,
the atmosphere of a derby match
the echoes of a legend around the pitch.

I shall put in my box:
the boos and jeers when the ref makes a bad decision,
the anxious moment of a penalty
the sarcastic cheers of an easy win.

I shall put in my box:
the questioning of a new signing,
the controversy of the Old Firm Derby
the screaming of a derby goal.

My box is made of gold
with starlight on the lid
the hinges are made of crystal.

I shall climb in my box
on the great wall of a ruby
then fall and land on dry water
the colour of the sea.

Mark Middleton (12)
James Gillespie's High School

LORD BEARER

Pride was my blood,
A gift from my creator
To be entrusted with my mantle,
To shower the altar with colour.

The community's trust
Is to bear their lord,
To betray him as he once was crucified,
To uphold his name.

To enlighten the dust
With a sigh of faith,
To resurrect belief in those that are lost,
To radiate warmth and forgive.

My heart lies in shards of colour,
To be treasure for the crows.
Pride was my blood.
I am bled.

Niall Dolan (14)
James Gillespie's High School

FISHERMAN

(After Mary Fedden RA)

The lighthouse on the cliff, squat,
Teeters on the edge.
Blue is the scene. Cold, wet
Waves crash like falling dustbin lids.
The old man staggers, only two toes
Catching fish, all damp and soggy.
The sun beats down on the lighthouse
On the cliff.
This way of life
Teetering on the edge.

David Grant (14)
James Gillespie's High School

WHY THE FRIDGE DOOR WON'T CLOSE

The fridge door won't close
And inside, things are happening . . .
And who are they after? Who?
Why, they're out to get you . . .
The pizza is friendly
But the oranges want to squeeze you.
The bananas are funny
But what do the berries say? *Boo!*
The lasagne is cheesy
But the pasta is crude.
The yoghurt is sweet
But the salad is rude.
The rice is nice
But butter makes you splutter.
The ham is with the lamb
But the peas shiver in your knees!
The tomato squirts you with juice
And the beef says *moo!*
The chicken clucks in
And the eggs break your legs.
Why does it happen?
It is weird.
And I know the answer
The magnets and the door are *broken!*
So when you sleep,
Don't forget to close the fridge door!

Vincent Chan (13)
Merchiston Castle School

An Evening To Remember

Christmas Eve,
as I walk in the front door,
I hear the babble of young children's voices,
excited as to what presents the next day brings,
I round the corner,
I see my young cousins,
arranged in a circle on the floor,
discussing in hushed undertones
what Santa is going to bring them this Christmas
I feel the warm glow of the fire,
flickering merrily in the grate.
As I go through to greet the rest of my family
I know that this evening,
is a moment to treasure,
an evening to remember.

Alastair Hall (13)
Merchiston Castle School

Shell Shock

The sandy beach surrounds me,
I kneel down on the sharp, pointy shell.
Blood gushes out like a fountain,
The waves crash around me.
I looked for the sharp shell,
That had split my leg.
I smelt the sea salt in the air around me.
In a panic I tried to stop the blood.
How was I going to get back to the boat?
The pain surged through me,
Head panic rushes around me.
It was a strange pain that I had never felt before.

Alexander Whalley (13)
Merchiston Castle School

Rock Jump

Climbing, cutting, hands and feet
for the ultimate exhilaration.
Jumping,
falling,
freedom,
yet safe,
no thinking, just falling into nothingness but
finding myself back on Earth.
I arrive
on a cliff, nothing in sight,
Just me, a rock and the sea,
I look down,
determined,
trembling, but not scared,
I see the sea,
nothing else,
I'm alone,
I have to jump,
free from thought,
I splash back to Earth,
start swimming with the cuts on my feet
stained in salty blood,
I retreat back to the beach,
but searching for nothingness.
Once again.

Alex Yates (13)
Merchiston Castle School

What A Brother

He has helped me for 13 years,
He saw my birth and my christening.
He has helped me in my work,
When I got lonely, he cheered me up.
When I laughed
He laughed too.
Now he is gone.

In the winter he took me sledging,
In the spring we went canoeing,
In the summer we played cricket,
And in the autumn we collected conkers
But where is he now?
He is gone.

I am growing up, but I still miss him.
Soon, he'll be back and we can shout.
Until then, I can only sit and wait.
He comes back at Christmas.
He says he has presents.
I can't wait.

Fraser Brown
Merchiston Castle School

Christmas

Christmas time is finally here,
A nice way to end a year of cheer.
Everything about it makes you happy
And makes you feel relaxed.

It is a good end to the year,
It makes you forget fears.
You forget all your troubles,
In the snow.

It is the best feeling,
Most are living,
To sit down and eat,
Christmas food at the table.

And when finally Christmas is over,
Everyone's finally sober,
And gets ready for
A Happy New Year.

Calum Russell (13)
Merchiston Castle School

DUFF SHOT OR SWEET SHOT?

I stood there on the first tee at Royal Dornoch golf course,
I was about to hit my first shot of my round,
Lots of rich Americans with their caddies gazed at me,
The whole club had dropped silent to see me hit this one shot,
I peered down the fairway only seeing bunkers and rough,
I smelt the fresh seaside air and gulped,
My hands began to sweat, my knees knocked and my heart skipped a beat,
My mind buzzing with the thought of mucking up
And the ball trickling off the tee and the crowd erupting with laughter,
I wiped my hands on my trousers fitted my glove and took a deep breath,
It was Common Entrance all over but this time twice as bad,
I stared at the ball took one more look at the fairway, then to my dad,
I began to swing and the lines my dad uses repeating themselves over and over
Again in my head, 'Straight back, Coke can finish, head steady,'
My heart regained strength when I saw the ball sailing down the fairway.

James Fearon (13)
Merchiston Castle School

The Christmas Picture

The shiny creases in the paper
Fill my stomach with excitement
And the butterflies start bouncing off
My insides again and again.
The ribbon lace is tightly tied,
So no unwanted early morning guests
Can break its seal.
The tree flashes and flickers as the
Fairies dance and act in complicating
Patterns which will never end.
The hanging jewels run all the way
Along the confetti.
The angel silhouetted at the top.
Embers spit from the blazing
Coal fire, and the Christmas
Spirit fills the room.
The snow blankets the Earth for as far
As you can see, and the night sky
Sits on top like a painting, as the
Stars shoot along its front,
Christening the special day.
Christmas morning has arrived.

Chris Fulton (13)
Merchiston Castle School

Ronson Cheng

I am playing McDonald's team on the pitch.
There were many people wearing football shirts and playing.
I can hear many people saying, pass or shoot.
I am kicking the ball.

I am thinking how can I score?
I feel very excited.
I shoot the ball into the goal.
And I score.

Ronson Cheng (11)
Merchiston Castle School

MUMS

Mums are good.
They make you treats.
They love you lots.
They give you lots of kisses.

They take you out.
They give you toys.
They help you when you are sad.
They help you when you are alone.

She lets you do whatever you want.
She helps you with your homework.
She gives you lots of sweets to eat.
She gives you money at the weekend.

She helps you when you are picked on.
She helps you when you are hurt.
She helps you when you have no clothes.
She helps you when you are low.

So, I guess that is what it is like.
Being a day-boy I mean
But me, I'm a boarder, and that's just fine for me.
Even though I miss my mum a lot, I wish I was a day-boy too.

Henry Dawson (12)
Merchiston Castle School

The Poé Tree

'Twas once beside the Poé Tree
That it did softly say to me,
'My leaves are green, my fruit is ripe,
So honour me and take a bite.'
Moving my fingers with a flicker of an eye
I noticed that, yes, I did spy
A devious look upon his face,
(Though it had none, I could embrace
A softened twinkle around his bough
Of futures not too far from now,
Of evil struck upon my form
That is not really of the norm)
So I did take one piece of fruit
And treated not unlike a lute,
I struck my hands across it figure
And spoke, 'I will not have you snigger
At a path you chose for me to take,
After I do this fruit's skin break.'

Archie Millar (13)
Merchiston Castle School

On The Roof

I am on the roof of my home looking straight out at the stars.
All I can hear is the traffic, which is slowly grumbling at the side
of my home.
The fresh breeze gently blowing against my face.
As I get slowly drawn into the night sky.

Suddenly I realise how amusing the universe is.
And it sends me into a relaxed and amazed mode.

Cameron Godfrey (13)
Merchiston Castle School

Scars

A field of grass and weeds. Long and green.
In front of the person I hated. Fists raised. Ready to fight.
Fear and anger contorted on his face. Throwing of bets on the fight.
The cheers, hisses, boos and laughing.
The touch of my fist, inflicting pain.
The smell of the flowers in the trees and the candy.
Thinking endlessly of the fighting, insults, and after the fight.
The anger welling inside, fists about to fly.

The fists fly.
I get hit and he gets hit.
Blood. Nails piercing the flesh of my cheek.
More blood.
The fight ends.
Him on the ground.
The scars stay forever.

Terrible.

Kiffin McGinnis (11)
Merchiston Castle School

Christmas Day

It is Christmas Day.
My brother and I stand and stare.
We see the tree with bells and all.
The music playing songs from the Lord.
I can touch my bike which stands in peace.
I smell the turkey roasting in harmony.
I want to ride the bike at once.
I can't express the joy in me.
I am so happy.
Christmas.

Laurence Evans (12)
Merchiston Castle School

The Swiss Alps

On the Alps
On a sunny morning
The fresh breeze
The smell of cold air
I walked up to a snow mountain
Then I thought, why don't I walk up it
So I did and at the top I slipped
Fell onto ice
Then a *crack*
The ice was cracking
My mum found me and said,
'Come on, let's go back.'
So off I went, in her arms
And in the end I thought
What a silly thing to do.

Duart Rankin (11)
Merchiston Castle School

The Long Haul

On a passenger plane, 35,000 feet high,
We are midway over the Atlantic.
Endless corridors of seats and hundreds of strangers,
Hundreds of conversations and the roar of huge engines,
The uncomfortable seat beneath me and the AC above me.
Plane food, sometimes travel sickness and hundreds of peoples' BO fills the air.
I want to get to sleep, but the distractions are too great.
Frustrated, hungry, restless, uncomfortable, tired,
I squirm on an itchy seat as I soar over the clouds
Exhausted.

Andrew Young (13)
Merchiston Castle School

CHRISTMAS

It was Christmas Day
When we were playing in the snow.
Our cheeks were glowing like red berries.

We were having fun like never before
As we were unwrapping presents, and
Playing with our toys in the glazing snow.

As we were getting sad as the time went past
We were saying farewell, goodbye to Christmas once again
We had so much joy like never before.

Before we knew where we were
It was time to go.

Jamie William Harris (13)
Merchiston Castle School

TO THIS DAY I REMEMBER . . .

It was the sort of event which was like a dream
I was put under the pressure of getting the kick
So there I was, standing, just me and the ball
Thinking, what if I get this
Or, what if I don't.
The more I tried to relax the more nervous I got.
But there was one thing that I could smell.
Glory.
I had one glance at the posts before
I took the five long, pressurising steps to hit the ball.
It soared through the air like a bird getting its prey.
I thought, yes, yes, yes, yes
But . . .

Hamish Locke (13)
Merchiston Castle School

CLEAR MIST

The luscious and cloudless landscape
Shattered by rags of bleary mist,
That hung like wet washing.
The lonely loch eager and ready for a deluge.
Then the rains come,
Drizzle at first, then downpour.
Moving over the mountains like a cat through water.
It moved cautiously and intimidatingly nearer.
Then, down it came,
As if being watered by a mammoth watering can,
For hours it came down.
To linger in this dreary, desolate, decrepit, dull, old house,
Seemed a lot longer.
It appeared as if someone was crying,
For a reason me nor you could fathom.
But still I tarried,
Craving for even a glint of rich, golden sunlight.
And still I tarried,
Then, over there a swift twinkle,
A sparkle beneath the balk of the great cloud.
A flicker of brilliant, crisp, golden light,
That could blind any and every mortal man.
Then I ran.
Ran as swift as an Olympic runner,
Dodged in and out of all kinds of obstacles.
I hurled the rusty old door open.
Finally, I was outside.
The sun hit my back,
And over by the hills, the most staggering sight,
A rainbow.

Neil Criggie (13)
Merchiston Castle School

NEW ZEALAND OF 1993

The year is 1993 and I was three.
The world was a big place for me.
It was going to be even bigger when
I heard I was going to travel halfway
Around the world.

On a busy day in May my family and I left.
I was very nervous not knowing what to expect.
The place was big to me and the toilets made
A funny sucking sound.

I fell asleep on the plane and the next thing
I remember is the smell of the fresh sea air
Waking me up in a strange room.
Then my granny came through.
I was confused but she took me
To my family and I could smell
The sweet smell of hokey pokey ice cream
Which they were eating.
The excitement of being in
Another country made me spill my
Orange juice.

The beach was smooth as you could
Feel the pumice rocks rubbing
Your feet.

Cherry Island was where you could feel
The silky feathers of the kiwis and
Hear them crunching on their food.

The city was big and you could
Smell New Zealand air and the
Faint smell of kiwi burgers.

Jordan Rennie (13)
Merchiston Castle School

Going Through The Gate

Walking through the gates
Wanting to make some mates
I knew it would be hard
But I just had to give it a go.

Feeling really nervous
Wanting to go home
Wish I could, wish I could
But I just had to give it a go.

Going into class the hardest thing of all
Thinking it would be really hard
He asked me a question, I did not know
But I just had to give it a go.

Wish I hadn't worried
I made lots of friends
I wanted to stay there
I did give it a go.

Jamie McIntosh (11)
Merchiston Castle School

New York

Firemen clearing rubble
Tears are flowing from eyes
Policemen clearing the area
Paramedics saving lives.

Ash and dust is everywhere
Tragedy has flattened cars
Shock and terror on people's faces
People from near and far.

Is this a horror movie?
We will never forget that fateful day.

Ross Garner (11)
Merchiston Castle School

The Beautiful Game

When I play football
I feel so alive.
It relaxes me and
makes me feel free
of my troubles.
If I am watching or playing
I just love the game.
Either winning or losing
I really don't care.
The best is when you play
with pals!
Having a laugh and keeping fit
This is why they call it
'The Beautiful Game'.

Michael Garrie (13)
Portobello High School

Seagull

Flying high above the sea,
Where no earthly troubles reach,
Through thunder, rain and flashing lightning,
To my roost upon the beach.
Raise your heads, earthbound creatures,
As you hear my screeching call
And wish that you could join me up here,
Just to escape from your squall.
To fly free, unchained into the sky,
Without any care or woe,
To be able to leave the Earth at will,
A joy that you may never know.

Ross McCabe (13)
Portobello High School

A Lazy Walk To School

Walking early in the morning,
Walking but not thinking about direction.
Awake but somehow still asleep.
In a light daydream
Like a lost bottle at sea,
Floating to nowhere.

The sight of people in cars
Rushing to work
Shouting and beeping
Like kids in a dinner line.
Walking past the bookie's
Seeing what the latest bet is
Debating over what the score will be.
The smell of the bakery
Drawing kids in for a bun
Like cheese to a rat.

Arriving at school
But not realising you are there.
Children in a group with bags
Like a soldier's camouflaged eyes.
The bell rings
Like an air raid siren.
All the children swarm in
Like the living dead.

Robert Scott (13)
Portobello High School

DAVE THE CINEMA SEAT

For 50 years I have sat here examining whoever sits near,
I have seen thousands of films,
Over loads of different eras,
I haven't really enjoyed a film as I find them so boring,
I would rather read a book, from what I've heard.

The worst day of my career so far, must have been April 7th,
On the premier of the new kids film,
A child came to sit one me,
His mum had a bag of sweets and juice,
Ten minutes into the film, the crumbs started falling,
Bits of chocolate and jelly beans aplenty,
Around halfway through the film, they brought out the juice
One of them dropped about half a can all over me,
This film better end soon, I thought.

In my long career I have seen many things,
Even some celebrities too,
But now I'm considering retirement,
I don't know how,
Maybe when someone sits down I'll just break,
But anyway I can't talk much longer,
The film starts soon,
Shhhhhh!

Tommy Sharp (13)
Portobello High School

THE TWO SIDES OF EDINBURGH

The grand opening of new shops, Harvey Nick's, designer names.
How are you going to buy one when you're selling the Big Issue?
Grab another latté from Starbucks.
Drop your change into the empty cup outside.
Watching a game of football is great!
Not when you've landed in hospital for going through the wrong gate.
Friday night out on the town.
Remember not to drink too much.
Bored of going to the same places over and over again?
That's no reason to get a criminal record.
The festival comes every year.
A chance to have a great day out with friends.
A carpet of litter is left behind, making the city grey and dull.

Rachel Miele (12)
Portobello High School

ON THE RADIO

Music plays out as many tune in,
Listening to their favourite songs.
In the car, in the house or at the football,
People listen with content.
The man on the radio reporting the news,
The disgruntled woman on a chat show,
Listeners laughing at Galloway's morning wind up,
While driving to work.
It always seems to be in the background,
Keeping us company when we're alone,
Cheering us up when we're depressed.
Like a supportive friend who's there to help.

Liam O'Neill (13)
Portobello High School

ROUGH STUFF

One day when I was in the park,
About half-past nine it was getting dark,
I saw a great big group of boys,
They were shouting and making lots of noise.
I tried to walk fast and out of sight,
I knew they were looking for a fight.
Thcy started to run, and so did I,
So fast I saw the trees fly by.
They were catching up, almost upon me,
When I suddenly thought, *how hard can they be?*
That was my first mistake, but here comes the crunch,
I turned right around and threw a huge punch.
This was not clever, no - not very wise,
Well not when the boy was three times my size.
He pushed me right over and I fell hard on my back.
I heart my head give a terrible crack.
The boys gathered round and started to kick,
This didn't feel good, it made me feel so sick.
I started to moan and I started to scream,
But then I woke up and it was all a dream.

Calum Cameron (13)
Portobello High School

WOOLLY HATS

Warm woolly fuzz,
Clasping at heat,
Warding off cold,
Keeping me dry in rain and sleet.
Easily spotted in the white fluffy snow,
Absorbing the little warmth,
Blocking out winter, as it passes.

Chris Smith (13)
Portobello High School

AUTUMN OR WINTER

Leaves on the trees,
Fall to the ground,
Fly with the wind,
Without a sound.

Red, green and yellow
Colours coming through,
Autumn is here
Leaves will remind you.

Trees are getting bare,
Winter's getting near,
Weather's getting colder
Sky's no longer clear.

Scarves and hats the fashion
Bitterly cold without,
Jackets worn, zipped up tight
You can hear winter shout.

'Hey, it's me!
I'm nearly here,
I'm going to bring the same old weather
I bring every year!'

Kirsten Fairweather (12)
Portobello High School

I Am A Leaf

I am a leaf
Up high on a tree
Watching the children
Down below me.

The late summer weather
Is turning me red
Making passing strangers
Raise their heads.

Now the air turns colder
And my sides curl in
Then all around
My friends turn thin.

I am all alone now
High in my tree
Winter gales try
To set me free.

Suddenly I fall down
Into the bin
Well now it looks like
Winter wins . . .

Nicola Schreuder (13)
Portobello High School

A Normal Winter's Day

Waking up in the morning
Tipping down with rain,
Got to go to school again
What a pain!

The darkness is lifting
While walking to school.

Winter's taking my energy
With walking up the stairs,
Carrying all the heavy books,
So tiring on the back
Winter's taking my energy.

A normal winter's day
Still tipping down with rain,
The darkness is coming
Walking home from school.

Elliot Britee (13)
Portobello High School

World War II

Bombs dropping overhead,
Sky is dark, people dead.
In my shelter I'm not quite asleep,
But still listening to people weep.

I play cards in my shelter,
Wishing I could slide down the helter-skelter.
Wondering how Lucy is getting on,
It could have been her house that was bombed.

An hour has passed I'm not quite asleep,
Still listening to the people weep.
I can't wait to get back home
And to call my friends on the phone.

Now the siren sounds all-clear,
The German planes aren't too near.
When will I go back again
To the place we call our den?

Kerry Henderson (13)
Portobello High School

PUFFINS

Waddling along with their top-heavy bodies
Colourful beaks wide open to make a tiny squeak.
Standing
Ready for take-off
They lift-off and swoop down the side of a cliff,
Black and white with whirring wings
Defying gravity, riding on the wind like a surfer on the water.

Landing on the waves, sending splashes like a fountain,
They bob along contentedly,
Paddling off in the doggy paddle if a boat comes too close.

They dive down into the sea
Then come back up with a beak full of sand eels,
Ready for that famous postcard pose.

Funny little birds with nests on grassy slopes
Like rabbit burrows.
They stand guard with dumpy bodies on bright orange legs.

Ruth Murphy (13)
Portobello High School

FORGOTTEN

Sitting on the highest shelf,
Too fragile to be touched,
Let alone played with.

Gaining more and more dust,
But no one knows,
As I haven't had a visit in years.

She keeps on staring at me,
Her big blue eyes twinkling,
She's up to mischief again.

She crawls over to my shelf,
Her chubby arms getting closer and closer,
She leans in for the kill.

Suddenly I'm no longer on my shelf,
But on the floor,
Cracked and broken,
But no longer forgotten.

Jenny McDonald (13)
Portobello High School

THE LONELY BUS STOP

A man stands at the lonely bus stop,
Waiting for a bus that may never come,
A battered case lies on the ground,
Bound with tape and string.

He paces up and down,
Looking for any sign,
Of life around the lonely bus stop
And sees none.

He ponders over past days,
Laughter and joy that is now faded,
The sensations of a colourful world,
That ended on this road.

His eyes stare unfocused into the distance,
Over the plains
And he wonders if anyone will ever come to the bus stop.
And relieve his never-ending watch.

Hannah MacDiarmid (13)
Portobello High School

Basketball Dream

The intensity in basketball
Runs through my veins
Like a player with a full head of steam.
The significant part of a player,
Is the heart.
Heart and soul is poured into a game.
My heart is the biggest part in me.
Follow your heart and it could lead to a magic place.

Basketball is my life.
My love for the game
Comes from four years of play.
When I grasp a ball
I play and play until nightfall.
My life's ambition is in my dream,
Everyone has dreams.
We all need dreams.
The dream to play basketball is from inside.
Inside the heart.

Duncan M Peacock (13)
Portobello High School

Otter's Tribulations

Water trickles calmly by,
Under the inquiring, radiant sun.
Silently the otter crouches,
Camouflaged in the overgrown grass,
Avoiding the predator's wrath.

Sipping gently by the river's side,
Still aware of the dangerous world around her.
Waiting to hear a twig snap or a leaf crunch.

Vigilant eyes glimmer with pride and dignity.
Protecting her young from the treacherous world.

Nearby the otter's mate is watching and listening,
For dangers as yet unseen,
Suddenly the biggest danger of all appears
Man!
Threatening to destroy the otter's world forever.

Karen Mackintosh (13)
Portobello High School

Circle Of Life

Bronze, flaxen leaves cascade off the trees,
As if shaken by a gigantic, hidden hand.
The masses of leaves move at the mercy of the wind,
Blowing in all directions, constantly metamorphosing.

Soon the forest shows signs of winter,
Frosted grass and frigid landscape.
Nothing stirs from beneath the ground,
All beasts await the morn of spring.

With spring comes the burst of new life,
Myriad of colours flood the landscape.
Buds spread like a burst of flame,
Breathing life back into the trees.

Summer covers the forest with its warm embrace,
Summer rain falls like gentle rose petals,
Caressing the awaiting plants.
Animals, birds and plants play and feed in this Garden of Eden,
Oblivious of the hardships to come.

Alison Mackintosh (13)
Portobello High School

Thunder And Lightning

A fast and dangerous spark of light,
Forked in the sky, a spectacular sight,
A sharp zigzag in the sky,
The voltage of power is dangerously high,
Fast and furious it shoots to the ground,
Static electricity without a sound,
It's amazing, but it's also frightening,
This electric charge, the bolt of lightning,
But in-between each spark of light,
There's a thunderous roar that's scary at night,
Like a bomb, with a noise to deafen the ears,
Though soon all is calm as the storm's end nears,
As the Heaven's open and the rain pours down,
It's like water from a tap as it plummets to the ground,
Now the storm has stopped and everything's silent,
Thunder and lightning can be very violent!

Hayley Duncan (13)
Portobello High School

FOOTBALL

Football,
Slick passing
Accurate shooting
Amazing athleticism.

Football,
Darting runs
Sky-high jumps
Big deflections.

Football,
Bad tackles
Fake dives
Coloured cards.

Football,
Fast breaks
Skilful players
Very expensive.

Football,
Clever attacking
Solid defending
. . . *Goals!*

Kara Gillies (12)
Portobello High School

Why, Oh Why?

I'm sitting in my French exam
What does 'Est-ce que vous' mean?
I want to get good marks
Should I look over my shoulder
And see what that boy's written?

I'm so tempted to look . . .
No! I won't, I won't!
My left eye just slipped
Why did I look at his answers?
Why, oh why, oh why?

The answer he has written
Is 'She looks'.
I don't think it's right
I thought it was in a question
Well, I'll put his answer.

Now it's two weeks later
I'm sitting in the hall
The teacher starts calling out names
Mine was the 36th
She walked so slowly over to me.

It must be bad news
Her fiery green eyes are staring at me.
She handed me the paper
49% 'Below Average'
It was the 'Est-ce que vous' one I got wrong.
Why, oh why, oh why?

Emma McCall (13)
Portobello High School

Cloudy Dreams

A little girl stares at clouds,
Observing unknown forms.
The objects slowly drift away,
Heading for the storms.

But some you might just recognise,
Like diamonds, mammals, clowns and fools.
Then the girl wonders,
Is that candyfloss or cotton wool?

They're just so fluffy, big and small.
They're snowy-white.
They look quite tasty,
Take a bite.

She flies away,
A magical world of her own.
Jumping clouds,
Comfy grounds,
Thinking, is Heaven really up here?

She comes back to her window
Watching boats, trees and little dogs,
Disappearing into fog.

So when the clouds come back,
Though far away they seem,
She will think that they are closer
And go into a dream.

Megan Spence (12)
Portobello High School

Colours Of India

Her eyes glitter and twinkle while deep in thought.
Hairline cracks like an old piece of wood
Colours she wears swirl and dance together
Bangles slink up her arm like a colourful snake
A golden sun hangs (broken) from her nose
A cloth of dazzling colours, drapes over her head.

Milly McGlone (13)
Portobello High School

Abandoned

They told me I was going away.
I thought I had done something wrong -
I felt guilty.
Abandoned by my own family,
No one in the world to care for me.
Nobody needed me.
I was just a sad, little ten-year-old.

The children's home was lifeless, dull
(A bit like how my parents described me).
I had no friends or family.
I was sad, felt useless.
I let out a long, angry, silent plea,
My pale cheeks were burning with anger.

When my parents left I was scared of the home,
Now I am scared of the world.

Kirsty Smith (14)
Preston Lodge High School

The Dragon's Lair

Edinburgh Castle: a great tyrant,
Sitting on a pedestal carved by a thousand icy hammers,
Lying in wait, smugly roaring at even intervals,
Announcing to the soldiers below:
Be worried, a dragon never sleeps.
Men frantically loading weapons, trying to tame the beast,
Looking up a vertical mile, through rock and vein,
Only to meet a fiery death.
Skin as thick as the Earth, impenetrable,
Protector of its kin, destroyer of its foe;
With many a man entombed in its belly,
A potent adversary feared by all.

Now the beast sleeps, dormant but not dead,
Its foes have long since gone,
A new race now exists in place,
Not foe, but rather a forced acquaintance,
The type with shopping bags and cameras akimbo.
It is now very much a multifaceted thing,
Allowing the drum to beat louder than its heart
And the men dance as long as the night,
A foreign flavour stolidly walking around bleakly unaware,
They are not walking on solid ground,
Instead a dynamic, living platform.

The beast is old now; unable to fight,
But is there any need?
It now relies upon being invaded by what it once called 'enemy'
It takes what it is given and makes life better for those around it,
Slowly encompassing and devouring,
Recuperating, preparing for the end of the year,

Where it shows its true colours.
But of course, truly it shines all the year round
It will carry on unchanged for perhaps another eternity,
Perpetually involved in its contemporary times.

Lawrence Middler (14)
Preston Lodge High School

LOCH NESS

One man stood alone
Next to the icy blackness
Staring. His reflection. His fate
He waited to be set free from this world
Free from his life of misery.
His condemnation.
An eighty year sentence
In the pits of Hell.
Waited.
He knew he had to do it now
Set himself free from this nightmare
And live in continual bliss.
He stared.
His face stared back
Closer and closer it came.

It hit him like he never expected
His face, his whole body
Felt like he had been skinned alive.
Soon, not to be, he thought.
Then suddenly, the thought froze.
As he fell deeper, it became blacker, colder
Blacker, colder.
Warmth.

Euan Metz
Preston Lodge High School

The Baby Is Dead

I sat all morning in the hospital waiting room
Waiting for my mum to come back
And tell me that everything was alright.

But each time she processed out of each room
The life and strength seemed to have been withdrawn from her
And worry and confusion had taken its place.

The last room my mum entered was small
With a scan machine in one corner
And a bed in the middle.

The door was closed and I was left outside
As if the nurses were more important
And cared about my mother more than I did.

As if they had known how she was feeling this past week
And had been there to reassure her
I felt shut out and alone.

The door was opened slowly
And I was beckoned in by the nurse
Slowly, I walked into the room.

Tears streaming from her eyes
I knew what it was,
'The baby is dead.'

I threw my arms around my mum and held her close
I could feel her pain, as I tried to soothe her
With comforting words.

The tears began to fall uncontrollably
As the reality of it all sank in
It was as if something hit me.

I looked her in the eyes
And told her that everything was going to be alright
But she looked straight back at me and said,
'My baby is dead.'

Patricia Blair (14)
Preston Lodge High School

Heggis: A True Story

I woke up in the afternoon,
Lying in a ditch;
A burning sensation in my arm,
Reminds life's a bitch.

It started with my girlfriend,
When I walked in through the door;
Something seemed strange when I saw her
And my best friend on the floor.

I should have kicked his ass,
And then smashed him with a golf club;
But instead I let them be and snuck away
To the cheap and friendly pub.

In the pub I was a raving mess,
Confiding in a chair;
The rest of the night must have involved
A bus to Motherwell and orange hair.

As I lay in the soiled ditch,
Fragments of the night return;
I realise that the scorching
Was a tattoo, not a burn.

Greg McEwen (14)
Preston Lodge High School

EDINBURGH CASTLE

It lies up the hill looking
Down on the huge city.
And everyone looking up gazing
At its beauty.
Amazed at its size and shape
Scared by its cannons

The one o'clock gun sounds
People hear the noise
And then they see the smoke.
They now know the time
It's time for lunch!

It lies on the dead volcano
But its history is still alive,
With battles and wars it
Stands alone on the hill
Still looking down

It looks down on the growing city
With its new stadiums and shops
As Princes Street packs with people
They forget about the castle.
They are dead at the dungeons
But alive at the Tattoo
It beats with the sound of drums and dancers.

It has seen change from old to new
It notices the night life and some new things too.
If it could speak it would tell us
But as it can't, it tells us by being there
Its guard on the city will not be broken
It is of course Edinburgh Castle.

Alastair Sutherland (14)
Preston Lodge High School

STRANGER

I remember her when we were small.
We had known each other for years.
In her class through years of school,
I thought I knew her well.

We were always together, never apart.
I'd always stuck by her when she needed me.
I was always there when she cried help.
We relied on each other . . .
Then.

I trusted her,
I was confused - felt sick.
How could I cope?

She felt guilty,
She felt lonely.
She needed me
It was clear.

It was hard after all those years,
But I knew I could never
Trust her again.
Now several years later,
When we pass,
She is only a
Stranger in my eyes.

Claire Stevenson (14)
Preston Lodge High School

Sky

The sky lit up brightly before us:
Blue, green, pink, yellow, ones we picked up and lit.

The garden looked like a dream.
Clouds of pink smoke hung around the grass.
It was a night we didn't want to pass:
Blue, green, pink, yellow, ones we picked and lit.

As one went out.
I went to light another,
Walking away from the children's mother.
I turned and watched their faces filled
With excitement and happiness -
They wanted to see,
Blue, green, pink, yellow, ones we picked and lit.

I stood back and waited and waited,
For we all wanted to see.
I began to get impatient, so fool that I am
I walk to the edge of the pond -
From where the magic came.
I look down from above,
Down to a glimmer of light, which suddenly
Became brighter.

Then all I could see was
Black, black, black, black, ones I didn't pick but lit.

Emma Muir (16)
Preston Lodge High School

DREAM

As the hearse rolled slowly forwards,
Past the field filled with red, red roses,
I looked to the sky
And quietly I began to cry.

It was my fault; I had dared her.
As I stood by the grave, it snowed peacefully.
The cold stung my eyes
And again I began to cry.

I remember her falling, in brutal flashbacks.
I never moved, never tried to help,
I could have grabbed her. I have to tell,
That I am so very sorry she fell.

I woke with a start; the sun filling my room.
'I'm going out,' she called, 'I'll be back soon.'
My eyes were still wet,
From the dream I'd just had.

I am confused. It was a dream I am sure
Reality flowed back to me. She's alive.
But the dream was so true,
Next time it could be me.

Dawn Hunter (14)
Preston Lodge High School

FEAR

I watch the world that passes by,
Whilst fearing every death.
No simple explanation,
For every stolen breath.
He takes them slowly one by one,
With not an inkling why.
I see them and I wonder
Why do they have to die?

I watch the world that passes by,
He takes them all away from me.
He helped them all upon that road -
And they tell me that they're free.
He has his reasons I've been told -
And I don't understand.
yet all those people that I love
Shall never hold my hand.

Kelly Peacock (14)
Preston Lodge High School

THE SEASONS

The fire mountain, is hot,
but in Scotland, it's not.
In England it's grand,
but not in New Zealand.

The slippery mud and watery sludge,
the rustling trees and beautiful breeze.

Now the water is still
and the landscapes are filled with
the sound of the wild
like it was a sweet child.

Michael O'Brien (11)
St David's High School, Dalkeith

Feeling Sad

Sadness is very black,
It tastes like out of date milk,
Sadness is the smell of dung
And a toilet that has never been cleaned,
It sounds like thunder,
It feels like belly-flopping in the pool.

Alan Knott (11)
St David's High School, Dalkeith

Fear

Fear is like a black hole
It's the taste of black coffee
Fear is the smell of someone breathing on you
Looks like the world's dead
It sounds like haunted music
Fear is far too scary for me.

Natasha Georgiou (12)
St David's High School, Dalkeith

A Witch

A witch is black
She's in winter
In a dark, eerie room in a blizzard
A black witch's cape
A big, black cauldron
She's in Hocus Pocus
Bats' blood and maggots' eyes.

Nicola Torrie (12)
St David's High School, Dalkeith

BLACK COFFEE

Depression is very black
The taste of burnt toast
Smells like someone's dead
Looks like an old grave
Sounds like nothing
Feels like the end!

Craig O'Donnell (12)
St David's High School, Dalkeith

ANGER!

Anger is bright red
anger is the taste of bitterness
anger is the smell of burning
it looks like an overgrown garden
anger sounds like a ringing in your ear
it feels like a rough wall.

Keron McDermott (12)
St David's High School, Dalkeith

FEAR

Fear is night-black
And has the taste of coal
Fear smells like mouldy eggs
And looks like a dead mole
I can hear it sounding like bubbling sick
It feels like a lump in my throat.
Yuck! Ick!

Luke Martin (12)
St David's High School, Dalkeith

Fear From A Kid's View

Fear is dark and black and grey
And tastes like slime and gunk
Fear smells of skunks nearby
And alleys are dark if you fly
It sounds like screams and cries of kids
It really makes me worried.

Becky Robertson (12)
St David's High School, Dalkeith

Love

Love is bright red
The taste of red strawberries
The smell of the fresh air
A garden full of red roses
It sounds like chill-out music
Love is so joyful.

Sean Walker (12)
St David's High School, Dalkeith

Fear Is Around Us

Fear is dark brown
The taste of rotten eggs
Fear is the smell of people running in terror
And it looks like people shocked in fear
The sound of people crying in pain
It feels like a black hole coming towards me.

Nicholas Naismith (12)
St David's High School, Dalkeith

Autumn, Reap The Harvest

Autumn brings the harvest fruit,
And brings the wind as well,
A multicolour spectacle,
Of leaves and a welcoming smell.

Autumn holds the greatest delights,
That many try to find,
The experience of autumn sights,
That opens up our mind.

Autumn brings the love of many,
The pumpkin and apple pie,
Young adolescents and children play in the leaves,
Through the window I espy.

But autumn is a chilling time,
For those who are in the cold,
The poverty, famine, tears and weeping,
By the homeless, young and old.

Oh some of us turn a blind eye,
And reap autumn's delight,
Some cower and shrink to the autumn wind
And ignore the poor's plight.

Oh we may eat the steaming pies
And hear the fond rustle of the leaves,
But for the people who are depressed and lonely,
They seek shelter in the dead trees.

So while you relax in comfort,
Beside your roaring flames,
Just think and feel for those,
That the cold autumn wind claims.

So, autumn wind I ask you this,
What will winter bring?
You have reaped the sorrow of many
And stole away summer and spring.

Robbie Ramsay (12)
St David's High School, Dalkeith

A Horse, A Horse
(Inspired by A Dug, A Dug by Bill Keyes)

Hey Mommy, wid yi get me a horse?
A big, golden palamino, or a wee black Shetland
Pony or a big broon Clydesdale
Hey Mommy, wid yi get me a horse?

Your no needin a horse!
How wid yi get the dosh ti feed it?
Your no getting a horse?

Hey Mommy, wid yi get me a horse?
I'd get a paper round ti keep it
Hey Mommy, wid yi get me a horse?

Your no needin a horse!
How wid yi look after it?
Your no getting a horse.

Hey Mommy, wid yi get me a horse?
I'd go up after school
Hey Mommy, wid yi get me a horse?

Hey Mommy, wid yi get me a horse?
Go on Mummy, get me a horse!
Alright, I'll get yi a horse!

Kirsty Rorrison (12)
St David's High School, Dalkeith

BEING BULLIED

Skinny, fat, whatever,
it really just can't last,
anyone who's getting bullied,
needs some help fast.

This bully needs some help as well
so you really ought to tell,
it really will clear your mind
and to the bully, you are being kind.

A teacher's one who can help you
a parent will help too
but the worst thing you can really do
is to keep it all to you.

Lauren Martin (12)
St David's High School, Dalkeith

MOTOR MAD

(Inspired by A Dug, A Dug by Bill Keyes)

Son — Hey Daddy wid you get me a motorbike?
A Honda or a quad to fly aboot the streets at night.

Dad — Dinnae bi daft yi cannae even ride a bike!
If I got yi yin it would be in 4 bits by noon the night.

Son — Hey Daddy get ies a m'bike. I could get your dinner fi the chippy at night. Oh Daddy piz get us a bike it would ge mi sometin ti day on a Saturday night.

Dad — Oright, shut your gob.
I'll get yi a bike if yi da the dishes after tea
Then I'll get yi a bike.

Colin Lapinskie (12)
St David's High School, Dalkeith

Happiness

Happiness is bright gold
The taste of strawberries
Happiness is the smell of flowers
And a field full of hay
It sounds peaceful and joyful
Happiness is exciting.

Natalie MacPherson (12)
St David's High School, Dalkeith

Luscious Love

Love is ripe red
The taste of newly grown strawberries
Love is the smell of red roses
And a field full of poppies
It sounds cheerful, like a wedding party
Love is luscious.

Dionne Ramsay (12)
St David's High School, Dalkeith

Love

Love is bright red
The taste of juicy cherries
Love is the smell of red roses
It looks like a bursting heart of love
Love sounds like a shooting star at night
Love is outstanding.

Rebecca Coull (12)
St David's High School, Dalkeith

A Fish, A Fish

(Inspired by A Dug, A Dug by Bill Keyes)

Daddy can u get mi a fish?
It's ma only dream
an ma only wish
aw, get mi a fish, will yi?

Whit! A fish
but fish smell
I hate their faces and hoo they swish their tail
Nut, ye're no gettin a fish.

But Daddy, they only 50 pence
I think they're cool
and they're no a big expense
Aw Daddy get mi a fish will yi?

OK
Will yi stop gon on,
Ye're nippin my brain
Ye'll get yin the morn.

Kevin Lucchesi (12)
St David's High School, Dalkeith

I See Red

Anger is dark blue
The taste of soap
Anger smells like a mouldy body
It looks like a madhouse
It sounds like death
Feels like you're going to burst.

Liam McHenery (12)
St David's High School, Dalkeith

A BEAR, A BEAR

(Inspired by A Dug, A Dug by Bill Keyes)

Hey Mammy, wud ye git us a bear?
Wi great big feet
'N' fuzzy-wuzzy hair?
Ah, Mammy git us a bear wud ye?

Whit di ye think this hoose is?
A flamin' zoo?
Whit else di ye want?
Some monkeys too?
Dinnae be daft!

Bu Mammy!
I wud ge I' somewhere ti live -
Under the stairs
I heard someone say
It's a braw place fir bears!
Ah, Mammy, git us a bear wud ye?

An whit ye di whin the toilet wiz done?
Aken whit ye'd di,
Leave it ti gid ol' Mum!
Ye can forget bout this bear!

Bu Mammy!
I sweat it wudnae be li' that!
U'd dae it ma sel',
In tha's a fact!
Please Mammy!

Alright, alright,
Fir the love o' Pete!
No need to bow!
Stop kissing my feet - I'll get ye a soft bear!

Caitlin McCron (12)
St David's High School, Dalkeith

A Poem To Friendship

When I'm down
She's always there,
To cheer me up
She never fails.

We gossip on the phone
For hours on end
And tell each other
Our deepest secrets.

We have our fights
On and off,
About stupid things
But in the end
We always talk.

We look into the future
And see ourselves,
Laughing and joking
About our past.

And no matter what,
We will always be
Best friends forever!

Oriana Andreucci (12)
St David's High School, Dalkeith

A Snake, A Snake

(Inspired by A Dug, A Dug by Bill Keyes)

Hey Daddy, geet us a snake
Theer really big and they've teeth tha' arnie fake
They eat loads o' mooses and they'd keep burglars awa'
And they widnae tear opp the furniture sae what wit ye say.

A snake! What if it breaks oot its tank
And sneak doon the stairs an eats yer brother Frank.
It'll eat the cat or chew up the dug
Or smash Mammy's favourite mug.

But I widnae be bad oor do anything wrong
And it is nae as bad as King Kong.
An' Daddy it widnae cost much tae feed
An there isnae much that it needs.

Dae ye think am crazy buying that blooming thing
Ye aint gettin' it, why no a bird that could sing
Or a goldfish or a hamster or a cute wee rabbit
Nae a snake, an' am nae bein' crabbit.

But Daddy please, it disnae get fleas
And it won't be like a cat and, get stuck in the trees.

OK Fine I'll get ye a snake
But it better no eat me oor yer Mammy for goodness sake.

Christopher Donoghue (12)
St David's High School, Dalkeith

A PARROT, A PARROT

(Inspired by A Dug, A Dug by Bill Keyes)

Mammy wid yi git eese a parrot
but no a noisy yin cause it wid nip ma heed,
I've been ofy lonely since my budge fell doon deed.

Away in byle yir heed yerny gettin a parrot
there's nae need.
It wid be some day ti yap ti and tell ma stories to.

That laddy's driven me up the wa,
Wantin me I by um a wee macaw.

It wid scwak all night and widnae be weesht,
bit mind you it wid keep him quiet at least
'Mammy a parrot, Mammy please.'
'All right then, where's ma keys.'

Kieran Davidson (12)
St David's High School, Dalkeith

THE BIG GREEN DRAGON

A dragon is green,
he is the summer.
In a cave
he is thundering.
A dragon is a coat of scales,
a big church bell,
a TV film,
a piece of meat.

Amie Rutherford (12)
St David's High School, Dalkeith

Sitting By The Window

Sitting by the window, thinking of you,
No one can do what you used to do,
You were the sunshine after the rain,
A helping hand and a cushion for me to land on.

I shed a tear or two, in memory of you,
No one can make me feel like you did,
You put a smile on my face, lit up the dark
And sheltered me from the rain.

When the hope had gone,
You gave me hope to carry on,
When the laughter had gone,
You made me laugh,
Nothing will be the same, there will still be a scar
But the love inside will burn for a million years and more.

Cheryl Hughes (12)
St David's High School, Dalkeith

Autumn

The trees move back and forth with the bare branches moving too.
The leaves scattered on the ground, red, yellow and orange.
The wind blows the leaves around. They flutter then fly away.
The birds go tweet, tweet, tweet and the squirrels scuttle up the trees.
The rest of the animals are hiding, they're watching all the time
The children come out to play in the leaves.
The children lie in the leaves, kick them and throw them in the air.
Then here comes the rain so they all run inside.
But the animals you can see peeking through a hole.
Then the rain goes off, so out comes the sun.
Then out come the animals and children all over again.

Caroline Johnston (12)
St David's High School, Dalkeith

A Football Ticket, A Football Ticket

(Inspired by A Dug, A Dug by Bill Keyes)

Daddy, can ye get ees sum football tickets for Saturday?
ta see Celtic beat Rangers,
or Partick an Hearts
Oh, Daddy will ye get ees sum football tickets?

I'm nay getting ye any football tickets,
they're tay expensive,
and it's tay far to go to Glasgow,
so no, yer nay getting any tickets.

But Dad, it's no tay far an no too expensive
ye'll enjoy the atmosphere
an the croods are always friendly,
aw, go'on Dad, get ees sum tickets will ye?

No! It's near ye birthday and we need tay save up
Oh, all right ye've bent me ear right enough
I'll get ye sum tickets.

Matthew Hathaway (12)
St David's High School, Dalkeith

A Bird, A Bird

(Inspired by A Dug, A Dug by Bill Keyes)

Hey Daddy, wid you get us a bird?
A wee budgie could learn to talk so I've heard
Ur a canary's sae pretty, I'd like one o they
Aw Daddy get us a bid. Will yi?

A bird! Are yi mad? It'd twitter awa,
An we'd have nae peace, the night ur the day,
Na, I doan't want ta hear another word,
Gae tae yur bed! Yur no gettin' a bird.

But Daddy, Ann ud gie us one fur free
An I'd clean it oot ya see
An Daddy, I'd pay tae keep iut masel'
Aw Daddy, get us a bird. Wull yi?

Nah, that's anuff, o yer greetin'
Jes stop yer repeatin'
Doan't yi sae one more word
Go on wi yi. Ah'll get yi a bird!

Bethan Rawlinson (12)
St David's High School, Dalkeith

A Cat! A Cat!

(Inspired by A Dug, A Dug by Bill Keyes)

Hey Mammy, wid you get us a cat?
a wee white fluffy yin, ur a big ginger kitten.
ur a really fat yin, ur a skinny we yin
aw mammy, get us a cat, will yi?

An whose cat'll it be when it pulls at the curtains?
an messes the carpet, and pees on the fleer?
it's me ur your daddy'll be tane for a mug
awa up the ster! an your no getting a cat.

But Mammy see wee Danny, is cat had kittens,
an is gien them away down the road
an honest Mammy, therr fur free
please Mammy, get us a cat will yi?

Ah, I'll think about it son
Actually come here and give me a hug
ah right a give in I'll get you a cat
Ah right!

Nicola McMahon (12)
St David's High School, Dalkeith

THE BEAUTIFUL GAME

Why do all men love football?
It's because it's a real man's game
All of the amazing football players
All that passion and pain . . .

Imagine the fabulous life you would have
All the money and being labelled a star
With a great new house with a pool inside
And having a Ferrari as your brand new car!

Imagine being a footballer, everyone thinking you're great
With your adorable kids and gorgeous looking wife
And imagine being a footballer
And imagine that wonderful life!

Daniel Stewart (13)
St David's High School, Dalkeith

SUN AND MOON

Sun
just comes
out of dark
new light shines on
Earth

Moon
shining
shining bright
shining star bright
night.

Grant Elliot (13)
St David's High School, Dalkeith

My Book

One day I'm going to write a book
and in it I'll tell all
everything that's happened I'm going
to recall.

You'll find one person cropping up
time and time again
this person's been so special
since I can't remember when.

And when my book is finished
you'll read it and you'll see
through this life that I have led
just what you've meant to me.

You'll find them at the start
right through to the end
I'll dedicate my book to them
for being my best ever *friend!*

Michelle Niven (13)
St David's High School, Dalkeith

Autumn

It's cold outside
and the leaves fall off the trees
I knew the day it was autumn
It was freezing and the wind was blowing
soon the snow will come!

I'm wearing a scarf, red and blue
with big long gloves and a snug hat too
include my shoes which are bright green
they make me walk like Mr Bean!

Mark Thomson (13)
St David's High School, Dalkeith

TIME

Moon
Appears
At darkness
Giving off light
Night

Sun
Appears
In morning
Shining quite bright
Day

Night
Is dark
Really dark
There is no light
Moon

Time
Goes past
Very quick
Tick-tock, tick-tock
Tick.

Dale Kierzkowski (13)
St David's High School, Dalkeith

LOVE

Love is red
Love is smooth chocolate
Love looks like Sean Crawford
Love sounds like romantic music
It feels like love is at home.

Rosheen Warnock (12)
St David's High School, Dalkeith

The Friendship

A tall, blue ship with sky-green sails
Puppies, kittens, rabbits with fluffy tails
This boat is huge, this boat is wide
Large portholes look out on every side.

Coloured paper, collages galore,
Card, ribbons, scissors line the floor.
Face paints, smell of happiness inside
Princesses play dolls and babies
Pirates capture children.

In the middle of this three children sit
Singing happily while they play
Wishing they could always stay
One is a rabbit, one's a bear
The other is a fairy with curly hair.

Alone they sing a song, it rings through the ship
From the bottom storeroom to the crow's-nest
Behind the bouncy castle, please sing it too
Those beautiful words, 'Arikambamboo'.

This boat exists in dreams of children
In every country and language too.
Turkey, India, Scotland, Peru
The ship hides among the glittering diamond stars
Still in the dark, happy feelings grow
They're still singing in their hearts the song they know.

Sarah McNeill (13)
St David's High School, Dalkeith

All Around I Sit And Stare

All around he sits and stares
Bobby, Jim over there
Bobby with his browny hair
Oh I wish I was over there.

All around he sits and stares
Lora, Jodi over there
Lora with her fluffy pen
Oh I wish I was over there.

All around he sits and stares
Jenny, Jack over there
Jenny with her freckly face
Oh I wish I was over there.

Across the room I sit and stare
Poor old Peter over there
On his own he sits and stares
Oh I wish he was over here.

All around I sit and stare
Come on Peter over here
Friendships made and hands are shaken
Now the first step has been taken.

Niall Grant (13)
St David's High School, Dalkeith

Her Sons

She never answered the door or telephone
For fear bad news lay beyond
Five boys she'd raised for four to die
And off to war the fifth had gone.
Hands smooth as pebbles worn down by sea
Cotton wool hair, skin loose on her bones
She sat, silence broken by a ticking clock
That echoed misery throughout her home.
Her mind, once a walled paradise of thought
A vivid world locked inside her head
Was destroyed by a hurricane of sadness
At the news her military boys were dead.
Her days were dark and time was heavy as stone
Her nights broken with nightmares of the war
The boys lying limp on enemy soil
For a cause they thought worth dying for.
Loneliness like frost in paradise set
Prayers in simple whispers of their names
Beneath the rubble that was the remains of her hope
Lay Peter, Andrew, Tom and James.
And once the news of John came after
The news that he was lost without doubt
The windows on the walls of her mind bricked up
And all the world was forever shut out.

Rachel Fulton (15)
St George's School For Girls, Edinburgh

THE TREES

They say there are fair folk there
High in the trees.
The trees tall, graceful and fair,
Swaying in the breeze.
Go for a walk,
The echo of laughter
The whisper of a song.
So calm, peaceful.
Hardly a breeze.

It's like the trees talk,
Leaning over,
Peering at you.
Exchanging gossip, singing a song.
You walk on through.
There is no noise.

Footsteps start to follow
Light and airy.
Like they're about to fly
Into the air.

You stop
And so do they.
Around you spin
And alone you are.
You hear a laugh,
It's just a joke
To the trees.
Or maybe the fair folk . . .

Far-off laughter, singing songs
Long, long gone.
Whispering trees,
Tall and proud.

They say folk live there,
High in the trees.
Many just laugh.

It's just a memory.
So it may be:
An echo of the past.
Just the whisper of trees.
But I know,
The fair folk live there.

Alexina Duncan (13)
St George's School For Girls, Edinburgh

ATTITUDE

No one understands how I feel,
No one can see what I see,
If you saw what I saw,
You might understand all about me,
You see, I have an attitude,
It's what makes me what I am,
What did you say?
You talking to me?
I know I have an attitude
So I will decide the way,
It's my problem
Nothing to do with you,
You think you're so perfect
Well I have news for you,
I'm going to decide what we do,
Can't you just leave it?
Can't you just let it go?
You made me like this!
You made me bad!
You made my attitude
It's up to me what I do.

Katy Campbell (14)
St George's School For Girls, Edinburgh

THE OTHERS

Boys and girls come out to play
Children's laughter, hey, hey, hey.

Others stay inside their house
Crouching down like a mouse
All they hear is shouting and moaning
But they try to concentrate
On the laughter of the children
Outside.

One day I will got out to play
One day
One day.

Darren Cornelius Beattie (12)
St Katherine's School, Edinburgh

MYSTERY

I didn't know you were there,
For a while that is.
I know now
I was scared, I still am
But I know now,
Everything will be alright
Only six months to go.

Then we can go home
And be forever friends.
I want you now,
But it's better to wait
Just be sure not to be late.

Lisa Scott (14)
St Katherine's School, Edinburgh

In The Graveyard

Lives remembered only by stones
Worn graves of forgotten souls.

Leaves rustling
Wind whistling

Sadness

Bones forgotten in a tomb
Rough walls so cold and alone

Dying in faith

So many secrets in the graveyard.

Amy Carroll (13)
Wester Hailes Education Centre

The Lonely Gravestone

The graveyard
So lonely,
The forgotten stay there,
Yet everyone tramples without a care,
Till the darkness comes.
Everyone laughs, jokes, sneers.
In the dark lurk all their fears
They haunt them, scare them,
Till the dark fades.

Heather Stevenson (13)
Wester Hailes Education Centre

IN A GRAVEYARD

Standing tall,
About to fall

Are tombstones
With shades and tones

Words inscribed upon a plate
Reading them with a mate

Crispy leaves lying all around
In a graveyard near the mound.

Walking round and round without a clue
About what to write for you.

Jonathon Callaghan-Thomas (13)
Wester Hailes Education Centre

FRIENDSHIP

You're my friend, no matter what
Anyone may say
1,000 miles or more apart
In my heart you'll stay
So thanks for always being there
And always by my side,
Because you're my friend, no matter what,
This time I'll decide.

Lisa Campbell (13)
Wester Hailes Education Centre

War on Iraq

War on Iraq
you felt it was coming
Bush and Blair teaming up
against the madman and chums.

Will he have nuclear bombs?
Nobody has a clue.
If he does you'd better start running
Bush and Blair too.
No action has been made
so Bush and Blair are safe.

Now we have the clues
it's up to us to decide.
Is it better to live in a dangerous world
than a safe one?
I think we know the answer.

Barrie Crawford (13)
Whitburn Academy

Chestnuts

C hristmas bells ringing in the church
H olly hanging on the doors
E ggs boiling on the stove
S anta's coming in a few hours
T oys and presents lying under the tree
N ice people bringing lots of Christmas cheer
U ncle Tom looking very well
T insel hanging on the tree
S ingers singing carols on the street.

Gordon Buchanan (12)
Whitburn Academy

Missing You

I can't tell you how much I miss you
I miss you more than words can say.
Every time I see your photo or piece of clothing
I breakdown crying,
Crying my heart out,
Wishing you were here by my side.

When I think of you watching over me,
It helps me so much,
Knowing you're there when I need you.

You'll talk to me when I'm lonely,
Comfort me when I'm down.

I miss you loads, Dad,
I love you loads,
I wish you could come back.

I'll never ever forget
What a wonderful and caring dad you were.

Hopefully, some day, somewhere,
We'll meet again.

Kimberley M Tait (12)
Whitburn Academy

I'm Different

People are different,
People are not the same;
Most people think I'm
Pretty insane.

People think I'm happy,
But sometimes I'm very sad;
People don't know me well,
They don't know I'm very bad.

I don't like some subjects,
Especially maths;
Sometimes I get very frustrated,
About multiplication paths.

I know people are different
And people are not the same
And I know that I'm
Pretty insane.

Alexandra Williams (11)
Whitburn Academy

WEATHER

R unning around in the rain
A ll wet and soggy
I 'm the only one out playing
N o one else comes out to play.

W e're all getting blown
I nstead of staying inside
N one of the parents come out of the house
D ads and mums all cosy inside.

S nowmen sitting everywhere
N oses made of carrots
O n their heads they wear a hat
W rapped around their necks, a scarf.

F rost makes your car turn white
R overs, Almeras and all
O ut of your mouth comes lots of steam
S parkling frost covers the ground
T he sun is high in the sky.

Susan Kelly (12)
Whitburn Academy

FRIENDS

Friends are like family,
Friends should be caring
And friends are for sharing.
Friends should be nice,
Like sugar and spice,
Friends should not row or fight.
You need your friends around,
To keep you company
When you're feeling down,
Friends are fun and you should
Have more than one.
Friends are like family,
Friends should be caring
And friends are definitely
For sharing.

Lauren Proudfoot (12)
Whitburn Academy

CHRISTMAS

C olourful decorations on the walls,
H eather hanging from the doors,
R oast potatoes on the tables,
I gloos standing on the roads,
S mall children playing in the snow,
T una salad on the go,
M others cooking for their family,
A nimals hiding from the snow,
S treets are filled with carol singers.

Christopher Fairley (12)
Whitburn Academy

TWO FEET AND FOUR PAWS

Two feet and four paws emerge, groggy but awake,
They grab themselves a breakfast snack and give themselves a shake.

Two feet and four paws walk through the morning dew,
They leave a trail behind them, just like a snail would do.

Two feet and four paws head along the river path,
Two feet throws a stick and four paws has a bath.

Two feet and four paws make for the forest trail,
Four paws is dripping wet, he really does smell stale.

Two feet and four paws go crunching through the leaves,
Through the brambles, roots and muddy spots
A new path they must weave.

Two feet and four paws are glad to be back home,
They start to snooze by the fire and dream of their next roam.

Kirsty McGraw (11)
Whitburn Academy

AUTUMN IS

Autumn is a wonderful time, so quiet and peaceful,
Autumn is colourful, leaves blowing in the cool breeze,
Autumn is joyful, children playing in the streets
with blue-coloured fingers,
Autumn is fallen leaves crackling underfoot,
Autumn is the known time between summer and winter.

Autumn is . . . here.

Megan Gilchrist (12)
Whitburn Academy

GRANNY

As I woke up at dawn,
I looked at the lawn
And I saw the buds drift away.

I then walked down the stairs,
To see what was there
And I saw my mother stand.

The tears dripping down,
As I made a frown,
For she told me my granny was dead.

I then fell to my knees,
As I shouted, 'Please,
Don't let this happen to me.'

I then looked towards the sky
And I screamed out, 'Why
Wasn't it me who passed away?'

I then took a deep sigh
And even more so I cried
And I prayed that it wouldn't happen again.

Chelsea Livingstone (12)
Whitburn Academy

MOLLY THE MOON

There once was a new moon called Molly
She was very bright and jolly
She smiled all night
Until the daylight
What a jolly new moon was Molly.

Danielle Harte (12)
Whitburn Academy

Autumn

Leaves falling on the ground as the trees become bare.
People cut the grass for the last time in the year.

Dark nights close in and mornings turn colder.
Jack Frost is out there.

Clocks ticking faster as winter approaches.
People wrap up warm.

Phil Baxter (11)
Whitburn Academy

Friends

F riends are forever
R ight there when you need them
I f you are ill, they are there for you
E very day you work and play
N ever-ending fun when you are together
D ancing, singing along with you
S o you need your friends.

Kerri Manson (12)
Whitburn Academy

Our World

Our world,
Dirt and death to some,
Oil to be harvested, coal to be mined,
But to others there's life and the sea,
Surviving for racial harmony;
Green and clean or black and grimy;
Which side are you on?

John Speirs (12)
Whitburn Academy

How To Make A Monster

The recipe for monsters
is very, very rare
you only get to know it
if you're really hard to scare.

A little bit of thunder
a crack of lightning too
a mouldy green sandwich
a smelly old shoe.

Mix them all together
and wait a minute or two
the ugly brown mixture
turns a shiny bright blue.

Put the mixture in the oven
and leave it overnight
open it in the morning
expecting a big fright.

He stands before your eyes
all big, ugly and blue
it's not your gran in disguise
it's a monster made by *you!*

Ross Keenan (12)
Whitburn Academy

When I Grow Up

When I grow up
I could be an astronaut
Up in the sky
Ever so high
Or I could work in the vet's
And care for your pets.

Maybe I could be a model
With my good looks
Or will I be an author
And write some books?
Well whatever I may be
As long as I am me!

Karen McLeod (11)
Whitburn Academy

My Friend Snuggles

I had a little hamster whose name was Snuggles,
He just loved getting lots of cuddles.
He unfortunately died of cancer
And I have a couple of questions I hope he can answer.

Are you free from pain?
Can you shelter from the rain?
Do you have a cosy bed?
Is your running wheel the colour red?

You were so small you could fit in my pocket,
You ran so fast, just like a rocket.
You had really long whiskers and long, fluffy hair,
Big, black, beady eyes which would often just stare.

The memories of you running in your ball,
Out of the living room, into the hall,
Remember the time when you crawled up my sleeve?
Your long hair tickled my nose and made me sneeze.

My friend Snuggles, I miss you so much,
It's just a pity we can't keep in touch.
You're in my thoughts, you're in my dreams,
We will always be together forever it seems.

Jamie Green (12)
Whitburn Academy

SECRETS

I am always proud,
When people tell me secrets.
It is hard to keep them;
You feel anxious to tell someone.
Sometimes they can be special,
Sometimes they can be nasty,
Sometimes it can be written down
And locked up in a box.
Sometimes people are tricked
By their conscience,
As secrets fall on others' ears.
I think to myself,
Should secrets ever be told?

Hawlie Lamond (12)
Whitburn Academy

WINTER WONDERLAND

Oh, I do love winter,
it makes me feel excited when I see the white,
sparkly snow.
I love the Christmas lights as I pass by all the
nicely decorated houses.
I enjoy building snowmen, it makes me feel creative.
I often lie and imagine Santa and his reindeer
slowly moving across the dark, midnight sky.
I love going outside in the morning and walking
on the white, crispy snow
and my cheeks and nose bright red.
I can't forget my tingly toes!

Shona Duncan (11)
Whitburn Academy

Burning Fire

It started as a small, flickering light,
Gradually the flicker grew vastly bright,
Nobody knew it would cause any harm,
If only they had a smoke alarm.

The flicker soon became flames,
Trying forcefully to break the windowpanes,
It greedily gobbled all in its path,
Leaving the room looking dingy with ash.

The fire spread quickly to the next room,
If they closed the doors, they'd be saved from their doom,
The house's windows looked like red, angry eyes,
They'll be miserable when they say their goodbyes.

Stephanie Duncan (12)
Whitburn Academy

Winter

I look out of my window,
The streets are white.
The snow always sparkles
In the presence of light.

I love playing with my friends
And having a laugh,
But when I'm too cold,
I'll get a hot bath.

But when winter's passed
And summer kicks in,
I'll play water fights
Under the warm sun.

James Neilson (11)
Whitburn Academy

Changing Seasons

The butterfly glides gracefully
On multicoloured wings
While caterpillars munch and chew
The bird gently sings
Sweet songs of love and peace and grace
Which no one can compare
The cygnets paddle near their mum
Slowly and with much care.

The leaves are falling off the trees
Yellow, orange and brown
Piles and piles of coloured leaves
Lying on the ground.
Autumn's passed and winter's here
For animals there is no food.
The birds are sleeping in their nests
All is quiet in the wood.

The sun has come, the snow has gone
To streams and fields of green.
Days are longer, dark nights past
And in the light, young plants are seen.
Spring has come, the birds return,
How seasons come and go
A few more weeks and skies are blue
Roll on summer, goodbye snow.

Megan Craig (12)
Whitburn Academy

Revenge

My brother chased me with a crab,
He found it by a rock,
But I will get my own back -
It's now in his sock.

I put a spider in his bed,
He screamed and hit me on the head
And next time you do that
You'll be dead -
He said!

Gary Swan (13)
Whitburn Academy

The Shadow In My House!

There's a shadow in my house,
I wonder what it is?

There's a shadow in my house,
Could it be a ghost!

There's a shadow in my house,
Maybe it's a monster!

There's a shadow in my house,
Hopefully it's my mum!

There's a shadow in my house,
It could be my friend!

There's a shadow in my house,
Possibly it's my brother!

There's a shadow in my house,
I wonder whose it is?

There's a shadow in my house,
Could it be, yes it is!

There's a shadow in my house
And it belongs to me!

Nicola Frew (13)
Whitburn Academy

THE NIGHT

The gleaming moon rises in the clear, frosty night,
The stars glow beyond it, showing an amazing white.
The fox and the owl come out to eat,
Poor innocent rodents, they happen to meet.

The darkness settles in, out in the winter's cold,
The large oak creaks in the garden, weathered, battered and old,
The icy wind rattles like a clatter of feet,
Swirling round lamp posts so dark in the street.

The snow starts to fall like dust to the street,
The ground turns to velvet, a carpet beneath our feet.
The gentle smoke spiralling from the fire,
Climbs up the chimney, rising higher and higher.

Come morning, the winter's sun shines once more,
The snow starts to melt drip by drip getting slower.
The milkman comes round and wakes everyone,
With a litre of gold top and a big currant bun!

Jonathan A Boyle (11)
Whitburn Academy

SCHOOL

The older kids say it's horrible, some younger kids too
Little ones say they love it, love it they do.
Getting into fights with a black eye and a bruise,
Making you want to lock yourself in the loos.
Big kids picking on you and taking your money,
Don't be ridiculous it really is quite funny.

Stephen Allen (12)
Whitburn Academy

Music

Music is invisible,
Invisible as the air.
You cannot see it,
You cannot touch it,
But you know it's there.

It enters through your ears
And it starts to swirl around.
It seems to fill your body
With its rhythm and its sound.

Music is like magic,
It puts you in a trance.
It sets your body moving
And makes your feelings dance.

Music is a mystery,
It seems to cast a spell.
When music really gets to work
Then everything feels well.

Clare Roberts (12)
Whitburn Academy

Autumn

Falling leaves come off the trees
Drifting through the air
Multicoloured crunching leaves
Underneath my feet
The street lights glow
As the dark nights come early
The air becomes cold as the children go to bed.

Gary Smith (11)
Whitburn Academy

Litter

L itter is just a mess
I t would be nicer if there was less
T o make the world a nicer place
T o put your litter in a better place
E xcept on the floor
R eally, we should have a better world to adore.

Allison McEleney (12)
Whitburn Academy

Yellow

What is yellow?
The colour of daffodils blossoming in spring -
The different hues of dying leaves in autumn,
A candle flame burning in an empty, dark room,
A calm, quiet beach next to the sea,
The hot, burning sun that lights up our world.
What is yellow?

Jeff Wilson (11)
Whitburn Academy

A Day At The Salon

Shampoo, condition, prepare for a surprise,
The magic she works before your very eyes,
Blonde, brunette, ginger or black,
The colours she does behind your back,
They twist and curl and tong your hair,
To give you a style that's oh so rare.

Elizabeth McLaren (12)
Whitburn Academy

Tiger

Wandering slowly beneath the tall, slender trees
Stopping every now and then to catch a scent on the breeze.
Finally his wish came true, he saw his dinner running free
Not for long he thought to himself, every chance I seize.

He crept slowly closer, closer to his goal
As his prey saw him he struck fear into its soul.
Sprinting, running, dashing, trying to catch his prey
But the prey runs faster so his hunger has to stay.

Wandering through the jungle, time to try again
Only God will know what's going through his brain.

Ian Sharp (11)
Whitburn Academy

Midnight At The Graveyard

Big, silver moon floating in the sky,
Watching silently as bats fly by
Witches and ghouls wait for me
Hiding behind an old, gnarled tree
Broken tombstones smashed and creepy
People in coffins, tired and sleepy
Old iron gates
It's a place that I hate
Don't go there after dark
Go somewhere safe, the pool or the park
Don't go there after dark.

Kelsie Huyton (11)
Whitburn Academy

THE NAGGING GIRLS

There are three girls in my class,
They nag!
They nag about fashion and passion,
They nag about the swimming baths and maths,
They nag about boys and their toys,
They nag about adults who fight and give their kids a fright,
They nag about boys who try to be funny and cute, fluffy bunnies,
They nag about the colour of pens and noisy hens,
They nag about me and our French teacher's name, Dee-Dee,
They nag about PE and my mate, Lee,
They nag about books and our RE teacher's looks.
The worst thing they nag about by far, is about jam being in a jar!

Callum Wilson (12)
Whitburn Academy

THE RIVER

A river is like a knife cutting through the Earth,
The sound of a torrent echoes across the land,
Louder than a brass band,
Its power ruling all,
Then it reaches the waterfall just to fall and fall and fall
And there at the bottom a calmness reigns,
Joined by many other water lanes,
Slowly so slowly the river grows slightly wider,
Carrying along wave riders,
The fish of course you silly fools,
Dodging the debris that is so cruel,
Then the seas begin to mingle with the river that is true
And the river's journey to its homeland is now through.

Billy Sharp (13)
Whitburn Academy

Come Back

Every night
I watch the stars,
Wondering when I'll
See you again.

It's been two years
And that's a long time.
Wish I could see you all
The time.

My friends think
I'm daft,
I go on and on,
That's because
I miss you loads.

When I'm all alone
I cry inside and
Shut everyone out
And try to hide.

I miss you loads
And that's a fact,
So please come back
Just one last time.

I miss you.

Ashley Rice (13)
Whitburn Academy

My Furry Feline

Soft and fluffy, cleaning her fur
Silent and sleepy with the occasional purr

Stretching and yawning, pricking her ears
Becoming alert to the sound that she hears

Fixed and staring, flexing her claws
Knowing with wisdom the fear she will cause

Watching and waiting, stalking her prey
Patiently anticipating dinner that day

Turning and pouncing, in for the kill
Then quietly returning to her warm window sill.

Ruth Burns (11)
Whitburn Academy